C000220525

# So Am I:

## What Teaching in A Prison Taught Me

by

**Merle Helen Morrow**

© 2011 Merle Helen Morrow
All Rights Reserved.

No part of this publication may be reproduced, stored in a retrieval system, or transmitted, in any form or by any means, electronic, mechanical, photocopying, recording, or otherwise, without the written permission of the author.

First published by Dog Ear Publishing
4010 W. 86th Street, Ste H
Indianapolis, IN 46268
www.dogearpublishing.net

**dog ear**
PUBLISHING

ISBN: 978-145750-244-6
Library of Congress Control Number: 2011934586

This book is printed on acid-free paper.

Printed in the United States of America

# CONTENTS

## PART II: Notes: Mid-July 2004 to July 14, 2005

To the students and tutors in Mrs. Morrow's SUI/GED class, with gratitude for their friendship and for the lessons they taught me.

To the memory of Mr. Leroy Hannah-Bey.

They are good, they are bad, they are weak, they are strong,
  Wise, foolish—so am I.

—Sam Walter Foss

# Acknowledgements

I began this project with the knowledge that I had to write a book, but without the vaguest notion how do it. I believe that if we move our feet, God will push us where we need to go, and a wealth of people helped me to do my part. I thank them with all my heart.

Thom Haller and Hannah Six, writing teachers who, along with my classmates, made me believe I could and showed me the way.

My writers' group, Writers by the Bay, whose criticism made it better and whose encouragement helped it to happen, with a special thanks to Don "Hack n' Slash" Campbell who read and edited and then read and edited again.

Sr. Patricia McDermott, IHM, God's angel and my spiritual director, who midwifed this project from conception to a long-awaited birth.

Drew Leder and Walter Lomax for their support and their willingness to read and review.

Warden Robert Koppel, one of the few people who know the origin of "the Cut."

The volunteer and professional first readers and editors who steered while I paddled and got this book where it needed to be: volunteers Greg Moore, Jim Moore, Paula Mineart, and Tianne Wheat; retired professional and always-and-forever friend Leigh Saavedra Thomas, professionals Melanie Rigney, who told me to do it the right way, Meredith Gould, and the people at Dog Ear Publishing who got it to its final destination with amazing patience and skill.

Jean "Pony" Moore, my sister, my best friend, and my very own cheerleader, along with Ben Moore, Scott Moore, and countless other friends and family, including the men associated with Mrs. Morrow's SUI/GED class, all of whom assumed from the beginning that I could do it. I can't begin to tell you how much that helped.

And, of course, Ciro, my husband and my rock, who has never asked why but has loved me through it all.

# AUTHOR'S NOTE

I did not keep a journal or take notes for the first year and a half I taught at the Maryland House of Correction, so the material in Part I came entirely from my memory. The material in Part II came from notes as well as memory. All of the stories are true. I've written only what I recall or have in notes and have not filled in memory gaps or created composites. The only facts I knowingly changed were the names of people who did not give me permission to use their real names.

I will donate all royalties from sales of this book to nonprofit organizations that serve the needs of at-risk children, people in prison, or people recently released from prison.

# INTRODUCTION

The value of a human life isn't diminished by the presence of evil within it. Sister Helen Prejean showed us this in *Dead Man Walking*. Truman Capote wrestled with the dichotomy while writing *In Cold Blood*, and the struggle nearly ripped him apart for years afterward.

Before I taught at the Maryland House of Correction, my beliefs fell somewhere between Sister Prejean's and Truman Capote's. I accepted that people were either felons *or* decent human beings, yet I wasn't comfortable with that belief. I was certain that we're all God's children but uncertain how that knowledge should affect my interaction with the rapists and murderers in my classroom.

My students taught me that no human being is exclusively good or evil, that good people do horrible things, that some people refuse or are unable to act out of the good within, that we can embrace the good without embracing the evil, and that redemption is a reality. These are our stories, as we exchanged the roles of student and teacher again and again, ultimately braiding a rope of understanding.

My part of the story began September 11, 2001, as I watched the unspeakable events of that day unfold on the TV in my hotel room. I was in a town several hundred miles from home, where I'd gone to conduct an investigation for the Department of Justice in a men's maximum-security prison. That afternoon I watched inmates prepare the prison chapel for a service for victims of the day's attacks and their families. Two inmates stood at a table, arranging wild flowers in Styrofoam cups and plastic tumblers, another walked over to put a cup of wildflowers on the altar, and a fourth straightened the rows of folding chairs. Their moods were somber and reverent, and my heart twisted as I realized that people in prison don't leave patriotism and compassion at the iron-barred entrance.

The image of the men arranging wildflowers stayed with me as we left the chapel and walked across the prison yard to the cell blocks. I thought, *The men in here are as devoted to their country as people on the outside, but many of them can't write an intelligible letter to us—their government—to ask for help. They're cut off from their rights as citizens. How will they ever get a job back on the streets?* My next thought was, *What are you going to do about it?*

On September 28, 2001, I left my job at Justice, intent on becoming a teacher in a men's maximum-security prison.

# PART I
## MEMORIES

## April 2002 to Mid-July 2004

Razor wire at the Cut

# ONE

Spring 2002
April

I put my purse, cell phone, and watch in the trunk of my green Camry, keeping my driver's license out for identification. And then, I took a deep breath of spring air and crunched across the gravel visitors' parking lot—on my way to interview for a job I felt was already mine. I crossed the narrow road and stopped in the employees' paved parking lot to look at the Maryland House of Correction, the prison commonly known as the Cut. The name had originated in the early 1900s because the train that ran between Washington, DC, and Baltimore had cut through the prison grounds on a sidetrack to deliver ice and coal. But few people knew that, and the name had come to signify the stabbings that regularly occurred there.

I'd seen the news stories about the stabbings. Fear and excitement fought for the upper hand inside me as I crossed the parking lot and entered the low, red-brick building that formed the entrance to the prison complex. Inside, the building had windowless, concrete block walls painted an institutional cream...more reminiscent of an infection than a dairy product. The faux pine scent of cleaning solution permeated the air. A walk-through metal detector and a short counter with a gray Formica top formed a barrier between two glass-enclosed work areas. A female corrections officer in a navy-blue uniform stood on the other side of the barrier. Behind her, in the left wall, a thick metal door hung on its track, waiting to be opened by officers in the glass-enclosed control center.

A tall man in a brown suit, white shirt, and beige tie smiled at me from beyond the metal detector and introduced himself as Monroe Fuller, the school principal. I assumed he'd recognized me from the description I'd given to the woman who'd made the appointment: five feet, six inches tall, blond hair, wearing a black suit and mauve blouse. He was slender, with caramel-colored skin, graying, short-cropped hair, and a military bearing left over from his career as an Air Force officer.

After the corrections officer patted me down and cleared me to go in, Mr. Fuller and I chatted and waited while the steel door screeched open across its track. The door clanged shut behind us, and we walked through its twin a short distance away and onto the grounds of the men's maximum-security prison. Two high, parallel hurricane fences topped with coils of razor wire surrounded the complex. The coils also covered the several feet of ground between the two fences, and in places they ran from bottom to top. The sharp edges of the blades embedded in the wire sparkled in the spring sunshine.

Mr. Fuller loped, and I trotted, along a paved drive that rimmed a grassy quadrangle and led to the main entrance of the prison building. Carved into the gray granite cornerstone was the year 1928. The brick walls were old enough to have the softness and charm of old brick, but they managed to look just dull and dirty. Tall windows topped with granite arches faced the quadrangle, and a rumble of inmates' voices escaped through the thick bars and steel mesh covering the windows.

In the lobby, two Naugahyde sofas sat against the side walls—one burnt orange and one harvest gold. Two drink machines sat against the back wall, but I never used them because I wasn't allowed to take money into the prison. Padlocked, glass-fronted cases hung above the sofas and displayed weapons confiscated from inmates. A control center filled the back left corner.

An officer in the control center opened a gate in the adjacent wall of steel bars, and Mr. Fuller and I walked through. The gate screeched across its track and clanged shut, leaving us in a cage made by the gate behind us and an identical one four feet in front.

The second gate grated open, and we walked down a long, vinyl-tiled hall to a flight of concrete steps, painted black with yellow reflective tape on the edges. The tape, dulled by shoes and dirty mop water, had stopped reflecting, and chunks of the steps' edges had broken away.

Halfway up the steps, noise crashed over us like a huge ocean wave, but it didn't recede. I stood in a sea of voices...inmates' and officers' voices blending into a loud roar. The noise never stopped, and I always met the crashing wave of it near the mid-point of the stairs. The steps led to an open area called Center Hall, where officers controlled gates that opened onto three wings of the building. An officer in the control booth flipped a switch and let us into another cage.

I chose not to look around after that because we'd walked into a hallway where inmates crossed from one wing to another, and I felt uncomfortable in their presence. We went through a third gate—so old that it swung on hinges and had to be unlocked with an enormous brass key—and entered the Flats, a long corridor with windows high above my head in the wall to our left and four tiers of cells on our right, most of them occupied. That wing of the building, built in 1879, housed 140 of the 1,240 inmates at the Cut.

The thought *Don't look directly at them* flashed through my mind, but I couldn't remember whether that applied to people as well as dogs. To play it safe, I looked only to my left, where Mr. Fuller walked between me and the wall opposite the cells. We made small talk until we reached a doorway in the wall, almost at the end of the Flats, and entered a narrow, windowless hallway that felt like a tunnel.

At the end of the tunnel, we walked through a gate and up ten steps to a second gate, which the female officer who was assigned to the school unlocked with her big brass key. Mr. Fuller introduced her as Officer Mason, and she let us through and locked the gate behind us. The school wing was cream-colored, but the doors were wooden, littered with pockmarks made by paint bubbles from years past.

Officer Mason's wobbly chair and small, battered wooden desk sat against the wall opposite the gate. Mr. Fuller and I turned down a hall to the left of her desk and immediately turned left again into his office. A small copy machine, a couple of wooden tables, and a few mismatched metal file cabinets lined his walls. An ancient air conditioner blocked the light from the window. Everything looked as though it had come from the back corner of the state's retired furniture warehouse.

Mr. Fuller pointed me to a stained, orange visitor's chair facing his desk just inside the room. He leaned back in his desk chair and said, "I'm looking for someone to teach a class on Tuesdays and Thursdays from four p.m. to six p.m. Mr. Bickford, the regional manager for State Use Industries (SUI), has funded a contract for a GED class for the men who work for him and want to earn a high school diploma. The regular school closes at three o'clock, before the men get off work, and they don't want to give up their jobs to go to school. The SUI jobs are the best ones in the prison."

Mr. Fuller continued, "We started this GED program last fall, but we haven't had a teacher for it for several months. Does that sound like something you'd be interested in?"

I didn't have the vaguest notion what he was talking about. I said, "It sounds great!"

He asked why I wanted to teach and particularly why in prison. He'd read my resume and knew I didn't have a day of education classes or classroom teaching experience…only experience with adult literacy tutoring, public speaking, and workshops.

I said, "At the Department of Justice, I supervised a unit that investigated complaints filed by inmates in state prisons and local jails, and I've read hundreds and hundreds of letters from inmates who tried to explain their problems and get help. Some of the letters were eloquent, but others were so poorly written they made little sense. Men and women who can't write any better than that have a slim chance of making it out on the street, and I felt a need to do something about it…so here I am."

He nodded and expounded on the need. I relaxed and felt I belonged there. After we chatted, Mr. Fuller walked me back to the metal detector. I walked on his left side so I could look at him without seeing the men in their cells. He said he'd let me know something soon.

The next day a woman called me from Ann Arundel Community College, which held the contract to provide a teacher for the SUI/GED class, and conveyed Mr. Fuller's job offer. I accepted.

* * *

On April 2, I drove to the Cut for my first day of orientation, walked through the metal detector, and stood with arms outstretched and legs spread while the female officer patted me down. She put a reinforced paper ID bracelet on my wrist and took my driver's license in exchange for a plastic visitor's badge I wore on a chain around my neck.

Mr. Fuller wasn't there, and the officer volunteered to call him. She told him I'd arrived then turned to me. "He said, 'Send her on up.'" Stunned, I fought with panic and didn't respond.

It probably hadn't occurred to Mr. Fuller, who'd been a flight navigator in the Air Force, that I wouldn't remember how to get to the school. But on the day of my interview, I'd stared at him to avoid looking at the inmates and hadn't paid attention to the route we'd taken...and then there was my horrible sense of direction.

Family and friends teased me about being directionally challenged, and I always countered with, "Well, I always get where I'm going...eventually." I probably would've gotten to the school that day, but the thought of what I might wander into if I took a wrong turn along the way terrified me. The terror must have shown on my face, because a male officer who was waiting for the metal door to slide open smiled and said, "Come on. I'll take you over there."

I appreciated the officer's kindness but hardly said a word to the man as we walked. Instead, I focused on memorizing landmarks, in case I ever had to find my way from the metal detector to the school on my own.

At the Flats, my escort yelled for an officer down a hall on our right to come unlock the gate, and then we entered the cellblock. The Flats had a musty smell that came home with me on the papers the men turned in and clung to my briefcase and the books inside. The concrete floor was sealed but not painted. It had turned a mottled, charcoal gray, and irregular, black cracks angled across it. On the right, floor-to-ceiling metal bars separated the corridor from narrow catwalks that ran in front of each of the four tiers of cells. The corridor was wide enough for three people to stand shoulder to shoulder across it, and it ran for sixty-seven yards. I'd never estimated distances well but was fairly sure of that one because the cells measured five feet wide, with forty cells to a tier.

High above my head, wires ran from many of the cells to the windows on the other side of the corridor, draped like crepe-paper streamers at a party. Later, I asked Mr. Fuller what they were. "TV antennas," he said. "There's no cable TV at the Cut. The men can have thirteen-inch TVs in their cells, but they have to buy them through the commissary for $200.00."

The officer took me down the Flats and turned me over to Officer Mason at the steps to the school. Once I was inside, Mr. Fuller and I sat in his office, and he told me that the inmates in the class had signed up voluntarily. He didn't say anything about the crimes they'd committed, but because that was a maximum-security prison, I knew I'd have murderers, drug dealers, and armed robbers in the classroom. I assumed the prison would ban rapists from the class to protect me.

Mr. Fuller said the tests of General Educational Development (GED), which the men had to pass to receive a high school diploma, covered six academic areas: language arts (that's grammar and writing for people of my generation), social studies, science, reading, and math. He handed me a list of the inmates' test scores, which showed they read at grade levels from below first grade to above twelfth grade. Math scores started at the second-grade level and went to the tenth.

I thought, *This is going to be a one-room schoolhouse! How will I manage all these grade levels and subjects at one time? I guess if the pioneer schoolmarms did it, I can do it, but I wish I knew how.* Mr. Fuller appeared not to notice my anxiety, but I didn't know whether he'd missed it or whether he'd become so desperate to find a teacher that even an anxious one would do. I knew that teachers from the outside didn't exactly line up at the gates to apply for jobs in prisons.

Right before I left, Mr. Fuller gave me a stack of catalogs and said, "Take a look at the test scores and decide which books you want me to order for you." I took the catalogs but had no idea how to make the selections. Back at my car, I put the catalogs on the seat and wondered why I'd believed I could do this job.

* * *

On the second day of orientation, I walked from the metal detector to the prison building by myself and, along the way, admitted that this was different from going into prisons for the Department of Justice. I thought, *Those other prisons gave me an escort, but I don't have any protection here.* And I remembered Paul, an inmate in a county jail who'd been my first adult literacy student in 1972. Over time I'd learned that Paul would do anything for his friends and family but that he had no more regard for people outside of that circle than I'd have for an ant on my picnic basket...maybe less. Still, anxiety didn't set in until the gate to the Flats clanged shut behind me, and it hit me that the men I faced didn't know me or care about me. I fell outside their circle of family and friends.

I told myself, *You chose to come in here, and you're going to have to deal with it. You can look at the floor and scurry through to the school, or you can accept that fear will get in your way and make you miserable. If you believe you're serving a purpose by coming here, focus on the purpose. Just go with it! You did it as a civil rights lawyer, and you can do it now.* That didn't help a lot, but I had a start, and the thought got me down the Flats and into the school.

I returned the catalogs to Mr. Fuller and confessed my ignorance. He smiled and said he'd select books for me. He also told me, "I've decided to separate the men into two classes. The ones who read at the fourth grade level and below will go to an adult basic education class that Ms. Treanor, a full-time teacher here, will hold in the afternoon. That leaves you with seventeen students."

Each of the seventeen inmates had a different test score, and I thought each one needed his own study plan. I didn't know I could group the men by skill levels, nor did I know enough to panic. We discussed the scores, and Mr. Fuller said, "Are you OK with all of this?"

I sat up straighter and said, "Sure, sounds like a fun challenge."

Mr. Fuller smiled.

Mr. Fuller stood up and said we'd walk over to meet Mr. Dan Bickford, Regional Director of State Use Industries, and to see the operations. The SUI building, located on the prison grounds, teemed with inmates who made license plates, furniture for state offices and universities, signs, plaques, mattresses, and uniforms, among other things. Mr. Bickford said the jobs paid between $1.10 and $2.35 an hour. He also said that the 300 men in those jobs were less than half as likely to return to prison after release as others.

We had to shout over the noise in the building, especially the noise from the machine that stamped license plates. The inmates, some wearing ear protectors, yelled to each other above the racket and went about their work, apparently inured to the din.

My orientation ended. I'd learned that I could get from the front gate to the school by myself; I didn't know enough to choose the books we'd use; SUI had a positive impact on the men; and Mr. Fuller expected me to teach six high school subjects, including math—the bane of my school years.

On my hour-long drive home, the full impact of what I'd agreed to do hit me. This was a bit more than the letter-writing class I'd envisioned. Suddenly I felt more like Dorothy in Oz than a pioneer schoolmarm in a cowboy movie.

* * *

My first class met on April 23. Driving to the prison that afternoon, I decided that—unlike the other teachers, as it turned out—I'd call the students *Mr.* and use their last names, both to model the respect I wanted them to show me and also send the message, "I'm your teacher, not your friend."

I'd assumed that some of the students had volunteered for the class to get out of their cells or visit with other inmates or do who knows what—pass drugs to each other or something. Still, I decided that to succeed as a teacher, I needed to trust the students and to think of them as fellow children of God. I'd need to try to see myself in them. If that meant I had to look directly into their eyes, then so be it. Besides, I assured myself, an officer would be in the room with me. If the inmates took advantage of my trust, the officer would rescue me.

At the Flats, the officer with the big brass key let me in, locked the gate behind me, and left. I would've been OK, but I saw two white inmates with shaved heads walking down the corridor toward me. I won't repeat the words that came to mind, but to a former civil rights lawyer from the Seventies, the men spelled trouble. To pass them, I'd have to either walk close to them on my left or close to the inmates behind the bars on my right. Some of those inmates rested their elbows on the crossbars and hung their forearms and hands into the corridor...and not an officer in sight. I toyed with the idea of going back to the metal detector to ask for an escort, but Mr. Fuller clearly expected me to get to the school on my own, and I didn't want to look any more unqualified than I already had. Almost within touching distance of the two inmates in the corridor, I decided to be my normal, Southern self, took a deep breath, smiled, and drawled, "Hi! How are *yew*?"

The two men jerked their heads back and stared at me, unsmiling. When they were even with me, one of them looked at the floor and grumbled, "How you doin'?" I let out the big breath I'd taken and said, "Fine, thank you," to their backs.

That had felt right, and I decided I didn't need to put a Kevlar vest on my personality in the prison. I'd act the way I did outside and hope that would erase the tension I felt from monitoring myself around the inmates. From then on, I smiled and spoke to everyone on the Flats, on both sides of the wall of bars, although, not wanting to overdo it, I did substitute "How you doin'?" for "Hi! How are *yew*?"

That day, Mr. Fuller, who usually left with the teachers around three o'clock, had stayed to introduce me to the class. In his office, he told me that some of the inmates would be absent. He said there'd been a mix-up, and the clerk hadn't put all of the students' names on the call-out sheet. I asked what that meant. He explained that the inmates weren't free to move around the prison. He had to send a list of eligible inmates' names to the cell-blocks, and the officers there issued passes for the school—like a hall pass in schools on the outside. I thought, but didn't say, that fewer sounded better for my first class anyway.

At the classroom door, I took a deep breath and prayed, "God, please help me to be a channel for your grace and to remember this isn't about me."

I don't remember much about the room, because we used it only that first day, but all of the classrooms had exceptionally high ceilings and barred, steel casement windows along one wall. All looked as though they'd been furnished from the same back corner of the warehouse as Mr. Fuller's office. Because the inmates in my class worked in the SUI shops, they'd showered and changed in the forty-five minutes or so they had between work and school, and the aromas of soap and men's cologne filled the classroom.

I hoped Mr. Fuller would hit a tangent—as I often did—postponing the time when I'd have to take his place in the front of the room. No such luck. He finished his introduction in what felt like a few seconds and left me alone with the inmates. The officer I'd assumed would stay in the room with me sat at his desk across from the gate, twenty-five yards down the hall and around the corner—I'd counted the floor tiles to measure the distance. The unarmed officer and I were the only people in the school wing who weren't convicts. I told myself that Mr. Fuller wouldn't leave me in a situation that wasn't safe, but my pounding heart kept my mind from hearing it.

Still not quite ready to look into the men's eyes, I turned to the green chalkboard behind the desk and wrote *Mrs. Morrow* in big yellow letters. I hadn't used *Mrs.* in my twenty-four years of marriage, preferring *Ms.*, but I wanted to make it clear that I had a husband at home. Everyone pronounced it *Ms.*, anyway.

Finally, I clutched my six-page outline, sat on the front edge of the desk, and looked directly at the men. Eight African-American men looked back at me with expressionless faces—except two men who smirked. The students sat, most of them slouched, in desks with mustard-colored plastic seats and dark-brown plastic writing arms. I guessed their ages ranged between twenty and sixty. Once I looked at them, I didn't see anything to inspire fear.

The inmates wore either blue scrub tops or white T-shirts and gray or navy sweat pants or jeans. *D. O. C.* had been stenciled in big black or white letters on the pants and scrubs. A couple of inmates wore baseball caps without logos, a couple of others wore kufis (crocheted skullcaps worn by Suni Muslims), and several wore blue cotton hats that looked like pillboxes, reminiscent of the style Jackie Kennedy had made popular in the 1960s. I didn't know whether the pillboxes had any significance or were a matter of personal style. One man wore a thin, white washrag on top of his shiny, shaved head.

I moved into lecture mode—a place that was familiar to me from the legal seminars and workshops I'd conducted over the years—and told the men that, based on their test scores, each of them would start in a different place, but they all could reach the same goal. I also said that every man in the room was capable of getting his GED or he wouldn't be in the class...something I believed at the time.

As I blathered on about homework and testing and the folders I'd give them to hold their papers, a man who slouched in a desk in the back of the room—one of the smirkers—yelled out, "What's this we hear about you being a lawyer?" Thus began my first conversation with a student.

I'd known that would come up eventually, the prison grapevine being what it is, and had prepared my response. "Yes, I'm a lawyer. I'm a *retired* lawyer. I've been a *civil rights* lawyer my whole career. I've never practiced criminal law, I know nothing about it, and I don't intend to learn, because I am *retired*. I'm glad you asked the question, though. That's something we needed to address up front." The inmates' smiles and chuckles said they'd gotten the message.

I finished with the items in my outline and said, "I need to get a writing sample from each of you to see where your skills are. Write at least six sentences saying who you'd be if you could be any person in the world—whether that person is alive now or not—and why you'd want to be that person. Be sure to include yourself among the possibilities."

Mr. Fuller had given me notebook paper, yellow pencils, and those skinny pens that come twelve to a box for the students to use in class. I put them on the desktop, and the men came up to get what they needed for the assignment. When they'd finished their papers, I handed the men standardized tests to take to update or establish their grade levels.

At the end of our two hours of class, the officer yelled something from down the hall to let us know it was time to leave. Many of the inmates still sat hunched over their desk arms, working on the tests. Mr. Wells, one of the two inmates employed by the prison to tutor in the class, collected the tests, and my students and tutors left the room. I stayed there for a few more minutes to pack up my briefcase, and realized I'd enjoyed my first day in the classroom. The men had behaved well, and I hadn't seen any suspicious activity. This just might turn out fine.

The next night after dinner, I graded the test papers. Mr. Fuller had given me a grading key, but it took me until two a.m. to figure out how to translate the test scores to grade levels and decide what each man's starting assignment should be. The process became routine in time, but I ended that night with tons of gratitude that only eight men had come to the first class.

* * *

The second day of class, two inmates walked toward me on the Flats on my side of the bars, and this time I felt only slightly nervous. The inmate with light-brown hair looked at me without expression, but the blond inmate smiled and said, "Hello, ma'am. How you doin' today?"

"Fine, thanks. How you doin'?"

After they passed, I heard the silent one say, "Who was that?"

The blond replied, "Can't you tell? She's a teacher."

"Is she your teacher?"

"No, but she's somebody's teacher, and she deserves respect."

I felt safer.

On the steps to the school wing, an inmate with a graying, bushy beard and shoulder-length, graying, brown hair stopped me. "Are you Ms. Morrow?"

"Yes."

"Well I'm just coming from Mr. Fuller's office. I'm supposed to be in your class, but I'm having a lot of family problems right now. I can't focus on school until I get these things taken care of. I hope you understand."

I said, "Of course I do," and walked on, thinking that was about the worst excuse I'd ever heard. I couldn't imagine what an inmate could do about anything happening with his family on the outside or how their problems could impact him in prison.

Mr. Fuller had stayed late again to introduce me to the men who'd missed the first class and give everyone a pep talk. When I walked into his office, struggling to juggle my packed briefcase and armload of loose books, he said, "Let me see if I can get you a file cabinet for your materials. I'll requisition one from the warehouse, but they'll have to send it to the shop for a regulation lock. The locks that come on those things do absolutely no good in here." I thanked him, and we walked to the classroom.

Mr. Fuller gave his pep talk to the sixteen students and two tutors in the room, and while he spoke, I looked around. The room belonged to the teacher who'd taught the SUI/GED class before me, and he'd agreed to let us share it. Officer Mason always locked all of the other classrooms before she left for the day.

The teacher's desk—another battered, wooden affair—sat in the middle of the wall to the left of the door, along with a dull green desk chair that wobbled and had casters that didn't work. At the desk, I faced the sides of the inmates' heads and, beyond them, a wall with barred casement windows. The inmates' desks faced a green chalkboard in the front of the room. Green chalk-boards also hung on the wall behind my desk and the wall behind the students. Torn, yellowed posters of the human digestive and cardiopulmonary systems filled the spaces between the chalk-boards, and a tattered world map overlapped the chalkboard on the back wall.

After Mr. Fuller left, I asked the new students, all of them African-American, to take a few minutes to write essays on who they'd be if they could be anybody in the world, including them-selves. One man boomed, "Including myself! If you knew the horrible things I've done in my life, you wouldn't no way think I'd want to be *myself*." There went my idea that everyone in prison claimed to be innocent.

With a twinge of trepidation, I walked around the room and gave standardized tests to the new students and the students who hadn't finished the time before. Then I called each man whose test I'd graded to come to my desk and discuss his results and his study plan.

While I talked to the students, Mr. Wells, one of the inmate tutors, worked on what I'd later learn was the manuscript for his second book, and Mr. Lee, the other tutor, worked on pencil sketches to pass the time. After the last student left my desk, Mr. Lee—a slight, wiry man with a graying blond ponytail and a leathery, weatherworn face—came to my desk to chat. His blue eyes crinkled at the corners, and laugh lines framed his mouth. Tattoos covered his arms from his wrists to someplace under his shirt. I didn't see any designs relating to death or violence, but I tried not to stare.

In the middle of Mr. Lee's tale about an adventure on his Harley, the officer yelled from down the hall. The tutors collected the tests and papers, and the inmates filed out.

"Good-bye, Ms. Morrow."

"See you Tuesday, Ms. Morrow."

I replied, "You take care now."

Mr. Wells stayed behind and straightened the classroom. He was fit, fifty-four years old, and five feet, eight inches tall with a medium-brown complexion. A kufi usually covered his close-cut, graying black hair. Deep parentheses enclosed his lightly mustached mouth, starting at the middle of his nose and curving down to his chin, pushing his cheeks into pouches even when he wasn't smiling. He was more serious than smiley but usually upbeat and occasionally playful, hiding a soft giggle behind his hand. His brown eyes sparkled on good days and looked dull and vacant on his few bad ones. Mr. Wells had arrived at the Cut about the same time I had, but it wasn't his first time there. He, like a lot of inmates, had been transferred between prisons several times.

I started a conversation to ease my nervousness over being alone in the room with him. "Mr. Wells, what is it that the officer yells to us at the end of class?"

"Oh, he's saying, 'Count's clear.'"

"And what does that mean?"

Mr. Wells told me that at seven a.m., four p.m., and ten p.m., the officers literally counted the inmates. Once the count started, the inmates had to stay in place and couldn't leave until count had cleared—until the number of men scheduled to be in an officer's area matched the number actually there, or until the officer accounted for the missing inmates. That meant no inmates could come into the school after count started. Also, no inmate in the school could leave until count cleared for the whole prison, usually between five forty-five p.m. and six thirty p.m.

The time of day that count cleared dictated dinnertime at my house on Tuesday and Thursday nights for the next three years and three months.

Over the weekend, I looked over the essays the students had written, expecting to read about the famous singers, sports stars, and other celebrities they all wanted to be. Only one inmate wrote that he wanted to be a famous anything—a singer and entertainer—but he didn't specify who. Two didn't have the skills to do the assignment. One wrote that he'd be a fireman, one a social worker, another like Noble Drew Ali (who founded the Moorish Science Temple of America), and two like Jesus. Four wanted to be themselves, and four wanted to be their fathers.

I had a lot to learn.

* * *

## May

At our next class, I could hardly wait to talk to Mr. Aloona about his test results. He scored high on reading, but his language arts scores hit the other end of the scale. In my years as an adult literacy tutor, I'd never seen such a wide gap in skill levels. I tried to figure out how that could happen and thought I'd come up with the answer.

The word that comes to mind when I think of Mr. Aloona is *quiet*, not *withdrawn* or *sullen*, just *quiet*. *Enigmatic* is the second word, but, in his case, I'm not sure that's a separate thought. He was forty years old, close to six feet tall, and rock solid, with a face that usually held no expression, except for his large, dark eyes. They reminded me of a fox's eyes: intelligent, sometimes playful, but mostly alert. He had a deep, soft voice and shy smile. Probably the most diligent worker in the class, he rarely chatted with other students. Much later, I learned that he was one of the few men I met who was serving time for a nonviolent crime.

Mr. Aloona sat in the chair next to me, and—certain he'd confirm the brilliant explanation I'd come up with—I said, "Is English your second language?"

With a hint of a smile and a puzzled expression, he said, "No, English is the only language I've ever known, and I *don't* do too well with *that*."

"Well, your reading scores are so high and your language arts scores are so much lower, I was trying to find a way to explain the difference."

It would've been a tiny smile if it had come from anyone else, but from him it was a big one. He said, "I can explain that for you. I taught myself to read after I came to prison, but I didn't know how to learn language arts."

"Wow! You taught *yourself*? How did you do that?"

He smiled a little broader at my reaction. "I ordered a paperback dictionary and some Westerns through the commissary. Most of the words in the Westerns were pretty easy, so I knew *some* of them. I looked up the words I didn't know and tried to figure those out. Then I wrote them down and memorized them, so I'd know what they were the next time they came up."

"That's *amazing*! How far did you go in school?"

"I went all the way to the eleventh grade and couldn't read. Isn't that something? They pushed me on through anyway to get me out. I would've graduated, too, but when I was a junior they started the tests that you had to pass to get your diploma. I couldn't read the tests, so I quit. When I came to prison, I knew I had a chance to get my GED, and I couldn't get it without knowing how to read. That's what inspired me."

My amazement at Mr. Aloona's accomplishment had barely died down when, several students later, Mr. Harris came to my desk—the only other person whose language arts and reading scores fell unusually far apart. Fifty-seven years old, Mr. Harris had medium length, grizzled hair and a large frame. He took pride in his developing pot belly and always wore a baseball cap, a man with a joke for everyone and a big smile that showed a missing right front tooth.

Mr. Harris started talking before I had a chance to begin. "I want you to know that whenever I get the chance to do me some overtime, I won't be here, and I hope that's OK with you. I feel like this here, I'll be getting out probably in four years, and I want to buy me an old piece of truck, something I can carry equipment in, because I'm going to go to school and learn more about welding. I know there won't be many jobs out there for me, with my age and past and all, but if I had me a truck and some welding equipment, I could get enough jobs to support myself and maybe save a little on the side. I'll need to have me a nest egg, and that's why I'm working all this overtime. I need to get my GED to get into welding school, though, so you can count on me being here in class when there isn't overtime."

I wasn't about to discourage his plan. I said that would be fine so long as he got someone to bring me his homework and pick up the next assignment for him.

Finally, I asked him about his test scores. He grinned all the way across his face. "Well, it's like this here. I haven't gotten a letter now for over twenty-one years, but when I first came in here there was some of my family would write to me. I couldn't read enough to know what they were saying, so I had to get somebody to read those letters to me. Now, that's not something you want to do in here because they wasn't doing it for free, and then they can get in your business too, so I made me a plan to learn to read for myself.

"I'd get the man to read the letter to me a time or two so I could memorize it. Then, I'd sit down and match up the words I'd memorized and the few little words I knew with what was on the paper, and that's the way I could learn the words I didn't know. The next time I saw those words I could read them, and I didn't forget neither. Problem is, I didn't have no way to learn about commas and things the same way, so I never did get them figured out. Anyway, my people quit writing to me pretty soon, and I didn't have nobody else to write to, so I didn't have any reason to know those rules."

He leaned back in his chair and grinned, and I told him he had every right to be proud of what he'd done.

Mr. Taylor-El came to my desk next. He was five feet, five inches tall and slender, with a long, narrow face and a mustache that reflected his forty-six years. Class clowns abounded in our room, but if I'd had to pick the lead clown, it would've been Mr. Taylor-El: the most vocal, the biggest cut-up, and the most vibrant. He bent double when he laughed and crinkled his almond-shaped eyes almost shut. Just as often, he smirked or grinned and cocked his head to one side. He wore one of the pillboxes, but you heard him coming, speaking to everyone he met, well before you saw his hat. He also was the person I noticed most often in the center of serious conversations before and after class.

After we discussed his scores and study plan, he said, "You want to know why I'm taking this class?"

"Yes."

"Well, my son was in [prison] boot camp, and he started working on his GED in there. He wrote me a letter, said he was having a hard time with the classes, and he was going to quit. I wrote back and told him, 'I'm going to tell you just like my father told me. Bad enough you're in there. The least you can do is take advantage of whatever they have to offer and try to better yourself while you're there.' He didn't say any more about his GED in his letters after that, and I thought I'd said about all I could.

"It was several months later, and I gots my mail on my way to that GED class they had before, and there was a letter from my son. I opened it when I got to class, and a copy of a high school diploma fell out. I just sat there and stared at it. I couldn't move; I was that surprised. And I sure enough couldn't talk to nobody or I would've lost it right there in the classroom. Then and there, I made up my mind that I'd do whatever it took to get my diploma so I could send a copy of mine's to him, just like he did me, and he could feel proud, just like I did. He doesn't even know I'm in school."

Driving home that night, I wondered whether I should have been so quick to dismiss the excuse the man on the stairs had given me about his family on the first day of class. Mr. Taylor-El obviously maintained a bond with his son. I admired Mr. Taylor-

El's efforts to be a good parent, regardless of the circumstances.

I also thought about Mr. Aloona and Mr. Harris and tried to imagine the determination and work it took for them to teach themselves to read, to imagine how lonely and difficult their efforts must have been. I thought about how much I admired them because they'd followed through and succeeded.

*Admired?* That surprised me. I'd prepared myself to deal with a range of feelings that might come up in my interactions with the men, but admiration hadn't been among them.

\* \* \*

My transition from lawyer to teacher happened quickly on paper, but it took the incidents of my briefcase, the star stickers, and the file cabinet to make it seem real to me. The catalyst for the first was Mr. Taylor-El, our class clown.

Eagle Creek made the favorite of all my briefcases, a brown, soft-side one, but I was self-conscious about taking it to school. I thought everybody who saw it would look at me as a lawyer...not a teacher. I wished for something else to hold all my stuff, but I didn't have anything short of a suitcase.

One afternoon in mid-May I walked through the gate to the school, and Mr. Taylor-El noticed my briefcase bulging with books and papers and rushed up to take it from me. He said, "You're going to hurt that little back if you don't start asking somebody to carry that book bag for you."

His comment stunned me for a second, but when I got in the car to drive home, I put my book bag on the passenger seat and laughed out loud. The change in terminology ended my days of feeling like a lawyer.

The second part of my transition came soon afterward, when I started using star stickers. My sister, a certified teacher, had included stickers in a teacher's start-up kit she'd put together for me. I looked inside the package and thought, "Yeah, right. I'm really going to put stickers on papers I'm giving to convicted felons!"

Finally, I decided that because she was a real, certified teacher, and I wasn't, I should trust her judgment, although, except for an American flag near the Fourth of July and a turkey around Thanksgiving, I worked up only enough courage to use the stars.

I returned the first papers with stars that May. The men looked confused and tried to figure out whether I'd used a color code for their grades. I hadn't, except on papers that had no errors and those that had only one. The ones without errors got a big "Excellent 100%!" and a gold star. A paper with one error got a silver star. On the other papers, I wrote "Excellent!" or "Very Good!" or "Good" or "This was a good try!" and randomly added a red, blue, or other colored star. I hoped my method wouldn't bring up the negative memories that the A-through-F system might. "After all," I thought, "I won't be sending any report cards home."

Most of the men were OK with the stickers; some coveted them. Some thought them silly but didn't let me know that until our next-to-the-last class. Miss Manners would have approved their graciousness.

Using the star stickers was a teacherly thing to do, but the transition piece happened when Mr. Lowery showed up after he'd missed three classes. Mr. Lowery, the man who'd asked me in our first class about being a lawyer, was forty-three years old and initially the only student who had a job that wasn't in SUI. He told me he worked out to keep in shape and stay healthy, and it showed. He was over six feet tall, had a shaved head, and a whisper of a mustache. A few of his upper front teeth were missing, which caused his upper lip to fold back on itself when he spoke…and he spoke a lot.

Soon after I started using the stars, Mr. Lowery asked if I could bring him a book so he could find an uplifting story for a talk he had to give at a church service. I hadn't been able to get the man to do any writing assignments, so I said, "OK, I'll bring you a book, if you'll promise to read it and write a report on some of the stories." He agreed, and I brought him *The Courage to Give* by Jackie Waldman and Janis Liebs Dworkis. He missed the next three classes.

The day Mr. Lowery came back, he returned my book but hadn't written his report. He sat at my desk, instead of yelling at me from his, and I knew something serious was on the way. He said, "I need to talk to you about my stars."

"What about your stars, Mr. Lowery?"

"Well, you know I've been out the last three classes. I had bronchitis; you can ask the principal. Thing is, while I was out, everybody else got at least three stars, probably more like six, and I shouldn't have to give up my stars because I was sick."

With Mr. Lowery, the hustle was a given, and I thought, *If I give him those stars, he'll run games on me to see how many stars he can get without working for them...but he does like his stars, and he has been sick.*

Compassion struggled with common sense, but the developing teacher in me settled the issue. "Mr. Lowery, you know I can't give you stars on work you didn't do."

"Aw, Ms. Morrow, that's not fair! It wasn't my fault I was sick."

"I tell you what. You give me some of those writing assignments you owe me, and I'll put double stars on those."

He chuckled and tried to hold back a smile. "Yeah, all right, Ms. Morrow." We both knew I'd never see those papers, but I felt like a teacher. Not yet like a faculty member, but that came when Mr. Fuller put my file cabinet in the staff room.

The school officer could see into the door of the staff room from her desk but couldn't see much of it, because most of the space lay to the right of the door. A wall with barred casement windows faced the door, and odds and ends of small battered tables and shelves lined the wall to the left. A cooler holding a bag of ice sat on one of the tables. A round table with an infuriatingly wobbly, plastic top and a desk chair with a back that collapsed toward the floor if you leaned against it filled the center of the room. A scratchy, burnt-orange, harvest-gold, and mud-brown plaid sofa adorned the wall to the right of the door, and a wooden credenza and cabinet stood against the end wall. A set of inboxes for faculty topped the credenza, and a small microwave, looking out of place in its modernity, sat on the cabinet. At the end of the credenza, a door opened into the staff restroom. It had ancient fixtures and a barred casement window with a ledge filled with pigeon nests and associated droppings that spilled into the room.

A sign on the door read, "Staff Only," but Officer Mason ignored it. She left between three p.m. and four p.m., when the shift changed and her replacement arrived, but we never knew who her replacement would be or whether they would enforce the staff-only sign. The inconsistency bothered me, so if a man came in to talk to me and the officer objected, I said, "Officer, I need him to help me carry my books to the classroom," which the men usually did anyway.

The day my almond metal, five-drawer file cabinet came, Mr. Fuller had it placed against the wall between the sofa and the door. A thick metal angle bar on hinges ran from top to bottom and covered the ends of the drawers on one side, held against them by a large metal hasp attached to the other side and kept in place by a padlock,. Mr. Fuller handed one key to me and said he'd keep the only other one.

As I put my things—lined paper, pens, pencils, chalk, books, my papers, and the men's files—in the drawers, students came in and said, "Look! Ms. Morrow has her a file cabinet."

"Whatcha gonna put in there, Ms. Morrow?"

"Yeah, that's nice. It's a pretty one, too!"

"Looks like new!"

When I locked my things in the cabinet after class, I felt like a faculty member—no longer an itinerant—my transition complete. I stopped thinking of myself as a lawyer who played teacher. I'd become a prison teacher with all of the joys and heartaches that might bring. That's the day it dawned on me that I could park in the paved, employee parking lot.

* * *

By month's end, we'd settled into our individual and collective classroom routines. Most of the men started their work as soon as they came in the room, except Mr. Taylor-El, who talked and joked with various people, and Mr. Lowery, who yammered at me while I checked the men's names on the roll sheet.

After I took roll, I'd walk around the room and return the men's work, tell Mr. Taylor-El and Mr. Lowery to get busy, and call individual students to my desk to go over the papers I'd just returned. The tutors, Mr. Wells and Mr. Lee, worked with the men at their desks, and men also came to my desk to ask questions.

The only blips in the routine came on nights when count failed to clear on time and we had to wait to be released. The first time that happened, we'd waited for about twenty minutes when Mr. Collins, a man who sat in the front of the room, said, "Ms. Morrow, we can't leave, but you don't have to stay up in here with us. You can leave any time you want to. Why don't you go on home and get your supper. We're used to this."

The other men echoed, "Yeah, you can leave."

"You go on home to your husband."

"You don't need to put up with this."

I was tired and hungry, but thought, *For the time we sit in this classroom, we're in this thing together, and I'm going to underscore our similarities…not our differences.* I said, "No, I'll stay until count clears, but if any of you are tired of working and want to get a book off of my desk and read or want to talk while we wait, that's fine." That also became part of our routine.

The books were on my desk because the file cabinet gave me a place to keep books for a reading program. I'd told the men they could improve their writing and their minds by reading—all true but not the only reasons I had started the program. I froze inside every time I thought of being imprisoned, but I couldn't let myself even imagine living in a cell without escaping into books.

The men gave me lists of their interests, and I got books I thought they'd enjoy. They listed history, cars, biographies, basketball, football, natural health, world religions, Harleys, real estate, novels, pool, weight lifting, camping, the brain and memory, and social issues. I haunted our local used bookstore and the used-book sale shelves of the library and bought new books to fill needs the used-book sources didn't meet.

The men signed and dated a three-by-five card to check out a book—one book at a time, with no time limit—and before most classes, Mr. Taylor-El returned a book he'd read and looked for new material. At first, when he returned a book we would joke around, then we started having conversations, and finally he and I developed a routine of our own.

After I'd corrected him several days in a row for disturbing people during class, he came to my desk with his usual strut that stopped just short of a dance. "Ms. Morrow, I gets antsy if I have to sit too long in one place, and I needs to take a break before I can get back to work again. Would it be OK if I come up here and talk to you every once in a while, so I won't bother anybody?"

"Sure, that'll be fine."

He must have meant he became *more* antsy after he sat too long, because antsy was a constant with him.

He came to my desk to chat only once or twice during the two-hour classes; he stayed no more than ten or so minutes, and it did seem to help him settle down. I saw his breaks as a solution rather than a problem.

Mr. Taylor-El struggled and plodded through his lessons, and sometimes the effort got to him. That's when he'd tell me he wished he hadn't wasted his school years. "Since I been grown, I realize that the teachers who tried to make me do the most work were the best teachers I had. My math teacher was hard, but I sees now he tried more than most to teach us what we needed to know." He shook his head. "Ms. Morrow, I was so scared in that class! I was afraid he was going to call on me to go up to the board and work a problem, and I knew I wouldn't get it right, and I'd be embarrassed, so I'd start acting out before I even got in the room, knowing he'd have to put me out. I got so bad, they kept me in art class all day so I wouldn't disturb my regular classes."

It had never occurred to me that people might act out in school on purpose, except to get attention. At least the art classes had paid off. Mr. Taylor-El showed me some of his pencil sketches, and he drew beautifully, but his art classes had stopped when he dropped out of school at the end of seventh grade.

Mr. Kingsley and I also developed a routine. At the beginning of class he'd come to my desk—not to chat, but for reassurance. Mr. Kingsley was thirty-eight years old and exceptionally intelligent. He was about five feet tall and had widely spaced teeth in a mouth that almost touched his ears when he smiled. He was muscular and stocky, his girth barely containing his coiled-spring energy. Without the smile, he intimidated me a little...like an unexploded bomb.

He'd passed everything on the pre-GED test except math, and he sailed through his math problems, until we got to algebra. The day of that encounter, he lost his smile. I explained the basic concepts, and he said, "OK, Ms. Morrow, I think I can do this.

Let me try." But still no smile. He worked alone for the remaining hour and a half of class, and his smile was back full-width when he said, "Good night." That became the pattern for the next several classes. I'd give him a little help and a pep talk to get him started, and he'd take it from there, working out a lot more for himself than I taught him. Between classes, he did all of his homework and sometimes additional work we hadn't discussed. I'd carefully avoided algebra since my first year in college a thousand years before, and I had to scramble to keep up with him.

When he didn't understand how to do the problems immediately, he'd bristle with frustration. Finally I told him, "You're not supposed to know how to do this work now. You're coming to school to learn how to do it, and you're doing *great*."

He said, "OK," but his tone of voice and look said, "That's a bunch of stuff!"—my first indication that platitudes didn't go over well in the SUI/GED classroom.

The men called Mr. Kingsley "Stump." At first, he glared when anyone used the nickname to get his attention. I thought he didn't like the name and waited for his reactions, afraid of what they might be. Then one day at the beginning of class, he slammed his books on my desk and said, "Stump can't do no algebra! I'm handing in my books." The nickname was OK, but he wasn't.

"What do you mean, Mr. Kingsley? You're doing *fine*."

"No, I'm not! I tried to do that next chapter, and I can't do not one problem. There's no point wasting any more time with it!"

I thought, *Oh, dear God, I hope he hit the snag before he got to the chapters that I haven't worked through. I don't want to lose this man while he's convinced that he can't do work I know he can do.* What I said was, "Let me see what you were working on." He showed me the page, and my heart sank. I hadn't looked at that chapter.

I took a deep breath and said, "Let's go over the material and see if we can figure out where you got off track," and to myself, "and hopefully I'll be able to remember how to do these problems as we go."

He said, "All right, but it won't do no good. This stuff don't make any kind of sense to me, and I can't do it. You'll see." I read some of the explanatory material aloud—playing catch-up for myself—and before I could finish or the man could even ask a question, the smile came back full strength. He said, "Oh, I see now! Let me go back and try to do that. Thank you, Ms. Morrow, I think I got it. Yeah, I got it now, Ms. Morrow. Thank you!"

Mr. Kingsley's confidence grew with success, and by the end of May he agreed to risk taking the GED pretest to qualify to take the GED exam. I put him on the regular school's list of students who'd take the pretest in June.

* * *

Also toward the end of May, Mr. Brandon joined us. Like Mr. Lowery, he worked outside of SUI, but I didn't bother to ask why he was in our class. Forty-six years old, he had a narrow mustache and receding hairline. The men called him Long-tall because he hit six feet, six inches. More than tall, he was big with broad shoulders—not plump or buff, just a big man. He had a wonderful sense of humor and a big smile that showcased a gold cap with a martini glass cutout on his left front tooth. He always kidded and greeted people, epitomizing the word *jovial*, although flares of frustration sometimes interrupted his joviality.

He had a fairly low boiling point, and, a couple of times, completely absorbed in doing arithmetic with his tutor, he shouted things out. The first time it happened, everyone was working quietly. Suddenly Mr. Brandon's big voice boomed, "Naw, m——-f——-, that can't be no seven! That's a eight!"

His outburst gave me a fit of the silly giggles. I knocked a pencil under my desk and dove after it, both to hide my reaction and to give myself time to straighten up enough to correct him. But the men immediately chorused, "Man, you don't talk like that in here!"

"What's the matter with you?"

Mr. Brandon said, "I'm sorry, Ms. Tomorrow. I'm sorry. I'm sorry. It won't happen again."

It did happen another time or two, but the men took care of it, and I behaved more like an adult. With this happy resolution, we sailed into June.

# TWO
## Summer 2002
### June

June began with good and bad news. The good news was that two months, to the day, after Mr. Kingsley started working on algebra, he passed the math portion of the pre-GED test and was set to take the GED exam. All of us shared his excitement, and his accomplishment encouraged the other men.

The bad news was that the prison went on lockdown, and we couldn't have school. During lockdowns, the men couldn't leave their cells...not even to shower or go to the phone, commissary, or chow hall. They got bag lunches three meals a day, usually a bologna sandwich, a small apple, and a carton of milk. Lockdowns also involved a *shakedown*, a search of the men's bodies, belongings, and cells to look for contraband. The administration imposed most lockdowns because of a stabbing or other infraction in the prison, and lockdowns lasted anywhere from a few days to a year or more.

I was grateful when that lockdown lasted only a few days, and even more grateful when the men told me the stabbing hadn't involved anyone in our class. My gratitude melted, however, when we returned to school and walked into the heat in our classroom. Classes ran all twelve months of the year, and our room on the top floor made the worst of the summer heat. The brick exterior wall had a heavy coat of plaster on the inside, and it absorbed—then emitted—more and more heat as the summer wore on, effectively turning the room into a kiln. To make things worse, the windows of the room faced west, and we got the full impact of the afternoon sun through the glass. I had to scooch my chair around—it wouldn't roll—to keep the sun out of my eyes.

The windows didn't open enough to allow any hint of a breeze, and the only air movement came from two oscillating fans mounted on the wall, out of reach and high enough to direct the heat from the ceiling onto us. Several times, the assistant principal told me to cancel class because of the heat, but I knew the men wanted to come to school, and I didn't want to let them down.

The men nagged me to bring a mug from home for ice water, and then they nagged me to get ice from the cooler in the staff room. "Where's your ice water today, Ms. Morrow?"

"You can't be up in here in this heat without your ice water." That touched me because the men weren't allowed to use the ice.

Even with the ice water, by the time I finished taking roll, my clothes had wet circles in the expected places, and drops of sweat ran down my face. My normally blonde hair—once naturally so— turned dark beige, and sweat dripped from the short ends of it to run down my neck and soak my blouse or dress. By the time class ended, I'd mounded tissues soaked with sweat and hints of lavender in the wastebasket next to me.

The lavender scent was there because I liked the men and wanted to do something for them. I couldn't bring treats of any kind to school as a lot of teachers on the outside do. Under prison rules, I wasn't allowed to give anything to the students or tutors, not even things not classified as contraband.

I'd remembered that Mother Teresa had said something to the effect of, "Do something, however small," and I'd started using lavender-scented bodywash and body lotion on the days I taught. At first, nothing else had come to mind. I'd read that the scent of lavender had a soothing effect and hoped it was true— anything to bring in a little stress relief. I couldn't tell whether it worked, but it was something I could do. Maybe it helped me to be calm.

\* \* \*

Around mid-June, I asked long-tall Mr. Brandon to read something to me and discovered that he couldn't read...not at all. Mr. Wells, one of our tutors, had taught adult literacy at another prison, and he agreed to work with Mr. Brandon, one-on-one.

Mr. Brandon couldn't read, but he was no fool and didn't want to be treated like one. I gave assignments to everyone for homework: interpretative writing, logic problems, grammar exercises. On the day I discovered Mr. Brandon couldn't read, I decided he'd be relieved if I let him slide—I knew he'd have to get help with the work from somebody back in the dorm—and I slipped by his desk without giving him a homework sheet. He boomed out, "Where's *my* homework?" I didn't do that again.

\* \* \*

A few classes later, while Mr. Wells straightened the room after class, he told me about his books. He said he'd written a book entitled *Narrow Vision*, in 1999, and gave me sheets with the name and contact information for a bookstore in Baltimore that had copies, in case my friends or I wanted to buy some. His ability to get a book written impressed me, and I did order a copy.

The book told the story of his life until he was sentenced to ten years in prison for bank robbery; he'd taken a historically high amount of money. That had been the conviction before the present one. On the last page of the book, he described the message:

> I sincerely hope after sharing in my experiences, you, the reader, *if not already*, will become more serious about your life and your future. You must realize that in this life, there really are no "shortcuts," especially when you compare them with the money one may obtain from hustling (as a shortcut) against the time one will do behind bars when caught. There is just no amount of money worth years of incarceration—**it never evens out**! (Emphasis and parentheses are his.)

Some of the things he wrote appalled me, especially those involving his attitudes toward women and the way he depicted robbing small stores, convenience stores, and banks as a career choice, but I admired his honesty. He made no excuses. In the epilogue to his book, he wrote that his "perspective of the lifestyle (he) was formerly living (had) changed," and he promised to tell about the changes in his second book, the one he worked on in class when he wasn't busy tutoring.

Mr. Wells made it his business to know as much as he could about the prison system and what went on inside it, so after I saw how up-front he'd been in his book—and after my curiosity nagged me to the point of can't-help-myself—I asked him about those pillbox hats. He said, "Oh, Ms. Morrow, those are crowns. Those brothers are Moorish-Americans. See, there's three Muslim groups in here: Moorish-Americans, like Taylor-El and them; Nation of Islam; and Sunnis—that's what I am. Most of the brothers start with Nation of Islam and then switch over to Sunnis. Yeah, that's what that is. The brothers with the crowns are Moorish-Americans. I thought you knew that. They got about forty members in here." He also told me that when the men joined the temple, they received either El or Bey as an honorific to add to the end of their names.

I'd had no experience with members of these religions and only knew what little I'd read, for example I'd gone online and learned that the "Moorish-Americans" were members of the Moorish Science Temple of America. Ms. Gelzer, the lead teacher at the Cut, told me she always liked to have Muslims in her classes because they kept things neat and didn't curse or let anyone else curse. I'd seen that in action when Mr. Brandon had slipped, although Christians had corrected him, too. I decided to wait and see what my new experiences would bring.

\* \* \*

# July

Early in the month, Mr. Adams-Bey and Mr. Hannah-Bey passed the TABE, the standardized Test of Adult Basic Education that measured achievement in language arts, reading, and math and qualified them to study for the GED...a big accomplishment, and both men had worked hard for it.

I'd graded Mr. Adams-Bey's and Mr. Hannah-Bey's TABE tests twice to be sure I'd gotten the scores right, and I could hardly wait to get to school and share my excitement with the two men and the rest of the class. Driving to school, I decided that the joy I felt over the two men's achievements might be enough to explain why teachers stayed in their jobs.

Mr. Adams-Bey, the man who wore a white washcloth draped over his shaved head, was thirty years old, muscular, and of medium height. He had a full mustache. Before each class, he pulled a desk into a front corner, away from everyone else, facing my desk and the rest of the men. I could almost hear him say, "I don't trust any of you." He rarely spoke, and when he did, he used as few words as possible. He didn't smile, but mostly glowered, with a look of defiance...not frightening, but off-putting.

Despite the glower, Mr. Adams-Bey did his classwork and didn't have significant problems with anything but math, although he had an occasional question about science, a subject he studied on his own. "Ms. Morrow," he'd ask, more as a command than a question, "what's osmosis?" He'd listen to my explanations and always say, "Thank you," when I'd finished, but without a smile. Still, a spark of something I found appealing flashed on occasion, something that said, "I don't believe I can do this, but I'm willing to trust you just enough to give it my best and see how it comes out."

Mr. Adams-Bey missed a few classes in July, and I asked if anyone knew why. Someone said, "He won't be back for a while," in a tone that told me I'd better leave it alone.

I asked Mr. Fuller if he knew anything about the absences. He said, "Any time the men tell you somebody won't be back for a while, you can assume he's locked up, and you can be pretty sure that's all the information you are going to get."

Mr. Adams-Bey was the first man in our class to go on lockup, a punishment limited to an individual, as opposed to *lockdown*, which involved the whole population. Lockup, or disciplinary segregation, used to be called solitary confinement. At the Cut, a write-up from an officer triggered a due-process hearing in which a hearings officer could impose the disciplinary segregation.

The administration had designated two tiers of the west wing to house men on lockup, and the men on lockup ate their meals in their cells. They could have basic toiletry items and religious materials, have one hour of solitary recreation each day, have one shower a week, and receive mail. They couldn't work, attend programs or activities, listen to a radio, watch television, or use the phone. Visits were restricted, and contact visits were denied; a man couldn't give his parents or wife a hug or a handshake.

A few weeks after his disappearance from class, Mr. Adams-Bey came back to class and, without a word to anyone, pulled his desk to the front of the room and got to work with his same intensity.

Mr. Hannah-Bey, the other man who'd passed the TABE, was in his early sixties. Tall and solidly built, he had broad shoulders and a strong, square jaw. A Moorish Science Temple of America crown almost covered his short, graying hair, and he had a slightly gray mustache above a sweet smile. His smile didn't do much to his mouth, but it puffed his cheeks and danced in his eyes. He spoke softly, as though taking you into his confidence.

In late July, Mr. Hannah-Bey handed me some papers and said, "Would you please take a look at this for me and see if you can tell what they're doing?"

"Sure. What is it?"

"It's the statement from the finance office where they send my pay. They've changed the way they do these, and I'm having a hard time understanding what they did with my money. It looks like I'm coming up short. They made a mistake with my money once before, and I'm afraid they're doing it again."

His confidential tone became even more so when he sat next to me. "See, I won't ever get out of here, so they're not supposed to hold back any of my money the way they'd do if I was going home some day. If there's a chance you'll get out, they hold some back and save it until you leave, but there's no reason to do that for me, and that's what it looks like they're doing."

The bank statement made no sense to me, either, but I felt far less disturbed by that than by Mr. Hannah-Bey's statement that he wouldn't be going home. Even in the heat, I felt cold when I realized this man with the sweet smile and twinkling eyes had no hope of being released. Mr. Hannah-Bey exuded calm, and I tried to do the same.

On my drive home, I gulped iced coffee from my thermos and mulled over Mr. Hannah-Bey's revelation. I was amazed by his lack of bitterness over having to live the rest of his life in the dreadful conditions at the Cut; having to guess which officers would enforce which rule which way from one minute to the next; being subject to the meanness of some of the officers and inmates, unable to resist it without being punished for insubordination or worse; being forever separated from trees and dogs and dancing. Forget bitterness. I couldn't imagine how he could hold on to his sense of who he was or to his sense of dignity—to his soul.

I knew Mr. Hannah-Bey and other men I'd met at the Cut turned to religion for guidance and sustenance, often for the first time in their lives, and I thought maybe that gave him the strength and comfort he needed to hold on and rise above his circumstances. I hoped that my faith would be that strong.

* * *

# August

The heat wasn't the worst thing the summer brought. Even though Mr. Kingsley had passed the pre-GED test, the school overlooked him when they made the list of qualified GED candidates to send to the state office. When the testers came to the Cut to administer the GED exam, he couldn't participate.

The state gave the GED exam on a regular schedule outside of prison, but at the Cut, they gave it only when enough men qualified to make it worthwhile for the trained team to administer it. Mr. Kingsley would have to wait four months for the exam to be given again. Mr. Fuller gave me the news. When I told Mr. Kingsley, he collapsed in on himself and murmured, "I'll take it next time. It's OK." But it wasn't.

Mr. Kingsley had been so excited about taking the exam, and we'd all been excited for him. I realized then that being a teacher can break your heart, too.

# THREE

## Fall 2002
### September

On September 5, I told the men that my husband and I planned to take a trip around Nova Scotia to celebrate our twenty-fifth wedding anniversary and I'd have to miss the next two classes. Their responses erupted, "That's great, Ms. Morrow."

"Happy anniversary!"

"You driving?"

"You gonna stay in a hotel?"

"You really been married *that* long?"

"Where is Nova Scotia, anyway?"

Mr. Kingsley went to the wall map, and I gave directions for his finger until it pointed to Nova Scotia. Then someone asked, "What're you going to see way up there?"

A few days into the trip, I decided to find something to take back to the men to say, "I thought about you while I was away," but I had to be careful about what I tried to take into the prison. The officers wouldn't let me bring in any food. I'd discovered that when I'd helped monitor an all-day test one summer Saturday and tried to take in a cold, sealed Gatorade.and an unopened granola bar for myself...no way. I'd had to take them back to my car, grumbling all the while.

I didn't find anything appropriate to take to the men until our last night in Nova Scotia, when Ciro, my husband, spotted a store during an after-dinner walk around Yarmouth. The store sold souvenir pencils—wooden ones, painted white and splashed with red maple leaves and *CANADA* in big blue letters. Perfect!

Back in class, I passed out the pencils, and the men filled the room with smiles and thank-yous. Some looked at their pencils as though they held something precious. Mr. Harris said, "This is one pencil that will never be sharpened!"

On the drive home that night, I thought how rarely I'd experienced that much gratitude in return for something so small. I knew the men gave me a lot of themselves, and I felt blessed by them.

\* \* \*

## October

Early in October, a new student, Mr. Clark, came to our classroom. Mr. Clark had a neatly trimmed salt-and-pepper mustache and a shaved head. At seventy-three, he was our oldest student, but only the wrinkles on his hands and on his light-brown face hinted at his age. He had a barrel chest and the physique of a fifty-something body builder. Either he worked out or his job kept him in good shape. I suspected both.

Mr. Clark worked in the uniform shop, where they made police and inmate uniforms, and he stood on his feet all day, operating the pressing machine. He once told me, "I can press two hundred and five pair of pantses in one day." His face and voice softened, and he beamed with pride as he said, "Those pantses is so smooth and nice when I finish. There's nary wrinkle anywhere."

Mr. Clark also beamed when he told me he had a high school diploma. "I don't need to earn my GED, but I been out of school for fifty-six years, and I don't remember all those things I learned, so I needs to do some more schoolwork. It'll help me when I get out." When I mentioned the diploma to Mr. Fuller, he said, "If he, at his age, wants to come back to school, then God bless him. Let him come. Mr. Bickford is fine with it, too." Mr. Bickford, the SUI Regional Director, often showed genuine concern for the men.

Mr. Clark worked as diligently at his schoolwork as he did at pressing pants. He was one of the men the supervisors occasionally kept to do overtime, but he always sent his homework in with someone and asked that man to bring him work to do in his cell.

Mr. Clark's enthusiasm made him a joy to work with and offset the only peeve I had with him—his refusal to see any point of view but his own. If he picked *A* as the answer to a question, it was hard to convince him that the answer should be *B.* One example of that trait made a permanent impression on me.

Earlier, in late spring, I'd realized that, between math and language arts, the GED students had no time left to study science and social studies, two subjects also on the exam. The full-time students had a separate class for each of those subjects, but I couldn't stretch our weekly four hours to cover the subjects. I decided to give a short lecture at the beginning of each Thursday class and at least teach the men the vocabulary they'd need to understand the exam questions...I'd start with anatomy. I wanted to get that out of the way, dreading the questions I imagined Mr. Lowery would ask when we got to the reproductive system.

In mid-October, the Thursday for the reproductive system lecture arrived. Not only did Mr. Lowery not ask embarrassing questions, nobody asked any questions at all. I'd begun with, "We're all adults here. We all know how babies are made, so I'm not going into the mechanics of reproduction. I just want to give you the vocabulary for the reproductive process and talk about the miracle of fetal development."

Most of the men looked at their desks while I talked, and the room stayed unusually quiet. That is until I said, "Except in rare cases, all multicell animals need to have a male and a female to produce an offspring."

Mr. Clark's hand shot up in the air, and with a smile, he said, "Now, now, now, Ms. Morrow, I know better, because I know about chickens."

"Mr. Clark, what do you mean, you know about chickens?"

"I mean you don't have to have a rooster to make a baby chicken."

"Mr. Clark! You know you have to have a rooster to make a baby chicken."

"Un-unh, now." His smile faded. "I grew up on a farm, and I know what I'm talking about. We had chickens, and those chickens laid eggs, and there wasn't nary rooster."

"Oh, I see what you mean. Yes, a hen can lay eggs without having a rooster around, but they won't be fertile. It'll be an egg you can eat, but it won't have a baby chicken in it."

"Nah, un-unh, un-unh." He shook his head and frowned. "Our chickens laid eggs and then they had baby chicks. We used to put something in the feed."

I smiled and struggled to hold back a laugh. "Mr. Clark, there is nothing in the world that you can feed a female of any species to make a baby. You've got to have a male involved in the process."

Mr. Clark didn't smile in return. "Not with a chicken, you don't. We used to put that stuff in they feed, and those hens would eat that stuff, and they'd hatch baby chickens, and nary rooster in the yard!"

"Mr. Clark, you've got to have a male and a female to make a human baby, and the same is true with dogs and cats and cows and squirrels … and *chickens*."

He raised his voice. "I know about all those others, but it's not true with the chickens, and I know that for a fact!"

Most of the other men sat wide-eyed and expressionless, swiveling their heads to look from Mr. Clark to me and back again as they followed our exchange. I thought, *Oh my goodness, most of these men grew up in the city, and they don't know which one of us is right.*

Mr. Clark was certain, though. Finally, I thought I'd found the answer. "You must have bought eggs that were already fertilized, and then you wouldn't need a rooster."

"Naw! Our chickens laid they own eggs, and we got baby chicks, and we—didn't—have—a—*rooster*."

"Well, I'm not going to convince you that you're mistaken, and you're certainly not going to convince me that a chicken can eat something that'll take the place of the rooster, so we'd better move on."

The men looked back at their desks, and I finished my lecture on the reproductive system. Mr. Clark had been so certain about his memory that I went online when I got home and looked up the reproductive process for chickens, embarrassed that I'd even consider doing such a thing.

* * *

My husband and I lived in the woods, and we loved the autumn leaves when they first turned colors and fell around our home…too early for thoughts of rakes. The colors blazed from the trees, peeked out of the evergreen bushes, covered the walkways, and took the place of flowers in the beds.

One of my favorite things to do in the fall was to walk through the colors and name them. On a walk that year, I named them for foods: omelet yellow for the maple leaves, butterscotch for the beech leaves, and papaya with streaks of lemon for the sweet gum leaves.

Before I could get any further with the names, a thought slammed into my head. *The men in our class haven't seen fall leaves since they went to prison!*

My search for the most beautiful leaves was on. I gathered them up and put them between the pages of an old phone book to dry while Ciro and I ate dinner. After dinner, I glued the leaves to sheets of plain white paper, two to four leaves to a sheet, and painted the leaves and stems with clear nail polish. The colors shone the way they would after a rain.

While the men took their seats in the classroom the next day, I taped the sheets to the walls, with long-tall Mr. Brandon's help—six above the chalkboard behind my desk, where the colors glimmered in the sun's rays, and six above the chalkboard in front of the men. As we taped, I heard a murmur go through the room behind me, and I turned around. The men's expressions looked a little funny—some heads tilted, a few smiles, some brows raised and others lowered. I said, "Oh, you won't have to write about these leaves, or anything. I brought them in for you to enjoy." That didn't do much to change the expressions.

A number of the men appreciated the leaves; a few were touched by them; many thought I'd gone slap crazy, but the leaves became a shared memory, one that we brought out and relived from time to time: "Ms. Morrow, remember the day you brought those leaves in here and put 'em all up on the walls?"

\* \* \*

Beginning in mid-October, Washington, DC; Maryland; and Virginia were terrorized by two snipers who drove around the area and randomly shot people. On October 24, news reports announced the arrest of the snipers, and the media began an ongoing debate over whether the teenage member of the sniper duo should be subject to the death penalty if convicted. I assigned the question as a writing topic for homework and expected to see papers in favor of protection of the young man and maybe a few anti-capital punishment essays. I'd assumed that the men would always come down on the side of the person who'd committed a crime. Mr. Collins destroyed that assumption.

Mr. Collins sat in the front of the room and faced the rest of the class. His head of short, black hair bent over a piece of note-book paper, shoulders hunched in concentration, almost hiding the hand that squeezed a yellow pencil. He put his desk there, but I never believed he did it to avoid the other men. When he wasn't bent over his work, a smile usually lit his dark, wrinkled face, and he joked freely with the men and me. He wasn't an old man— forty years old when I met him—but his frequent smiles had left their lines.

Mr. Collins had strong, but not inflexible, opinions, and he didn't hesitate to voice them. After I made the writing assignment, he said, "If that boy did what they say he did, then he needs to pay for it. Don't make no difference how old he is. He didn't have no business killing all them people. He's just the same as anybody else."

Many of the other men agreed with Mr. Collins, even though they knew I didn't.

On the drive home, I mentally growled at myself. *You still haven't really accepted that those men are individuals, that they run the spectrum politically and every other way. Why can't you realize that!*

\* \* \*

# November

The thick walls had given up all of their summer heat, and the ancient radiators failed to take up the slack. The men switched from T-shirts and scrubs to sweatshirts, and I began to shop for cardigans, wool blazers, and wool pants to augment the radiators' efforts. I didn't mind the new outfits and could deal with the cold a lot better than the heat, but I felt bad for the men. They couldn't run to the mall to get warm clothes.

Around mid-November, Mr. Clark, our oldest student, handed in his work at the end of class. Rubbing first one hand and then the other, he said, "Ms. Morrow, I'm sorry my script's so bad today. I just hope you can read this. My hands got hurt real bad in the Korean War, and some cold days, looks like I can't get them to do right."

"This is fine, Mr. Clark. I can read it. Did you serve in Korea?"

"Yes, ma'am, I went overseas with the U.S. Army." He told me the name of his unit and outfit and where he'd fought. "I'm a good citizen, Ms. Morrow. When I got back home from the war, I started working for (a national, private hospitality company that served the Federal government and private industry), and I was with them for thirty-five years, until I was fifty-four and came in here. They was always asking me to work big, important events where they needed somebody they could count on."

I gave "ooh"s and "wow"s and tried to look appreciative and impressed—as I certainly was. I also tried not to show my surprise over his history.

I knew that other men also came from less-than-impoverished backgrounds. Mr. Wells had told me about his grandparents who owned a dry cleaning business where his mother had worked.

During one of his breaks at my desk, Mr. Taylor-El told me, "You know, I gots four sisters, and me the only boy. All of them got their high school diplomas, some got their college degrees, and me, I never even been inside a bookstore. You know, my mother keeps all those diplomas." Another time, without any hint of his usual bravado, he told me, "I don't have no excuse for being in here. I comes from a good family and a good home.

Before my parents retired, they both had responsible jobs. My father was a supervisor, and my mother had a top-secret clearance. They both made good money, and they always stuck by me. I don't have nobody to blame for this but myself."

Mr. Clark, Mr. Wells, and Mr. Taylor-El raised an issue that I'd thought about a lot, and I mulled it over as I drove home through the winter darkness. When I told people I taught at the prison, they usually had one of two reactions. One group viewed people in prison as evil convicts who deserved nothing but contempt, and the other viewed them as poor, unfortunate people who'd had such horrible childhoods and lives that they "had no choice but to turn out the way they did."

I knew the group that held contempt had no clue as to who populated the prisons, although they were right to think of *some* of the men as dangerous, and I decided that the second group were well-intentioned but just as far off the mark. I tried to think of ways to tell people, beyond my family and friends, about the men's individuality. Ideas rolled around in my head, but I couldn't find one I thought would work, nor could I find a way to address the problems the misconceptions caused.

I couldn't fix the problem Mr. Clark had with his hands, either, but I remembered the "do something" quote and got pencil grips and ergonomic pens for him. They helped only a little, but you couldn't tell that from his response. He came into the next class with a big smile on his face. "Oh Ms. Morrow, those things you brought me last time helped me a lot! I can do better now. Yes, ma'am, I'm much obliged."

I tried to find more-effective things to do, but I couldn't. Finally, I stopped the search and consoled myself with the thought, *Well, at least he knows somebody cares.*

\* \* \*

Mr. Collins, who usually squeezed his yellow pencil in the front of the room, missed the first weeks in November. The men said he'd asked them to tell me he had a problem but would be back soon. The day he returned, I noticed he'd gotten thinner and I said, "You've lost some weight, haven't you? Looks good."

He leaned over my desk and looked directly at me with eyes devoid of their usual sparkle. "You know, since I been in here, I have an immune problem, and it's starting to take hold. I can't keep weight on me any more. I'm not feeling too good, either. That's why I've been missing classes. I may have to miss some more, from time to time."

Talk about feeling like an insensitive fool!

"No, Mr. Collins, I didn't know that. I sure am sorry. Of *course* I'll understand when you have to be out. You need to take good care of yourself, now."

From then on, it was as though the man were melting. He'd never been plump, but his wrinkled face, once full and glowing, became cadaverous. Still, he bent his head over the lined paper and did all he could to squeeze the right numbers out of that pencil. He asked me if he could work on his essay-writing skills as well, and I said yes, but he missed a lot of classes after that and wrote only sporadically.

* * *

Also in mid-November, Mr. Adams-Bey, of the white washrag, passed the pre-GED test. Our joy over his success brightened the winter gloom—until he missed several classes in a row and the other men said he "wouldn't be back for a while." He was on lockup again. I asked Mr. Fuller if he knew how long Mr. Adams-Bey would be locked up. He said, "I'll see what I can find out."

The next week, Mr. Fuller stayed at school on Tuesday to tell me what he'd learned. "Adams-Bey will be locked up for five months. Now, when somebody's locked up that long, it usually means he'll be ineligible to go back to his SUI job, so he'd also be ineligible to come back to your class. I'll see what I can do, but don't get your hopes up."

I was heartsick, certain that Mr. Adams-Bey could have passed the GED exam. He'd worked so hard, and I hated to see the opportunity slip away from him.

* * *

The unfixable problems mounted, so I was almost relieved when a problem came up that I could fix. Mr. Taylor-El and Mr. Nichols had stopped handing in their classwork and homework, or more likely had stopped doing it. Mr. Nichols was twenty-six years old and slender, with a rectangular face, large brown eyes, short hair, and a neat mustache. I learned later that, according to his sentencing judge, he fit the horrible-childhood assumption.

I needed to confront the two men outside of class and give them a do-it-or-else lecture, but thought, *These men are felons who've done no-telling-what to no-telling-how-many people, and I'm not so sure I want to risk making them mad at me.* I considered asking Ms. Gelzer to stay with me while I gave my talk but didn't want to chew the men out in front of her. Finally, frustration over my inability to fix the other men's problems drove me to address this problem head-on.

On my drive to the prison, I rehearsed and re-rehearsed my speech, and before class, I called Mr. Taylor-El and Mr. Nichols into the staff room, one at a time, to deliver it. Wearing my displeased-teacher look, I said to each, "I'm tired of sitting down to correct papers and not finding any work from you. You've got a good mind, and there's no earthly reason you can't get your GED, but you have to do more than want to. You have to do the work! If you decide to work, then I'll do everything in my power to help you, but if you keep on going the way you are right now, you'll waste classroom space and my time. I *know* you can get this GED, but it's your call. If you decide to stick with it, then start handing in your work, and we'll get the thing done."

Each man nodded in response—his face without expression—said his own version of, "I know you're right. I'll start doing better," hung his head, and left the room.

I mentally kicked myself and thought, *These are rational adults who recognize a justified rant when they hear one. I've done it again! I imagined Mr. Nichols and Mr. Taylor-El as the universal felon with one depraved mindset. The first problem I need to fix is my own!*

Mr. Nichols started doing his work right away. Mr. Taylor-El missed the next two classes. I thought I'd lost him, but he came back. Afterward, both men always turned in their work, and other men who'd occasionally skipped assignments quit skipping them.

\* \* \*

Facing the problem with Mr. Taylor-El and Mr. Nichols prepared me to deal with an issue that arose soon afterward. Mr. Fuller told me that if Mr. Kingsley passed his GED exam in December, he wouldn't be able to graduate with the Class of 2002 in January as he should have. People at the state office in Baltimore graded the tests, and they wouldn't finish in time for graduation. Mr. Fuller gave the news to Mr. Kingsley before class.

In the classroom, Mr. Kingsley waved his arms, paced the back of the room, and stormed, "That's it! I'm not putting up with any more of this stuff. I'm not waiting all that time to go to no graduation ceremony. They can just put my piece of paper in the mail, because I'm not going to graduation after this. I'm *finished* with this school. If we wasn't locked in here, I'd leave this school right now and never come back!"

I went to his desk in the back row, both to be closer to him, hoping the lavender fumes and I could calm him down, and to put myself between him and his audience. I faced him with my back to the rest of the class, and he sat down. He'd told me earlier that his parents looked forward to the graduation ceremony, so I said, "Mr. Kingsley, what about your parents? You don't want to disappoint *them*."

Still sitting, he raised his voice, "They don't need to see me graduate. I've got five brothers and sisters, and every one of them has a high school diploma. My mother has all their graduation pictures up on her wall. She don't *need* another one."

"Mr. Kingsley, I'm a mother, and you'd better listen to me. Do you know what your mother sees when she looks at that wall of pictures?"

"Yeah, she sees *successes*."

"That's probably true, but what burns in her heart is the picture of the child that isn't there."

We looked at each other for a few seconds, and he dropped his head and said quietly, "OK, I'll think about it."

I didn't know whether I'd said and done the best things for Mr. Kingsley, but I did know I hadn't been afraid.

\* \* \*

I'd beaten my fear, but I learned on the Tuesday before Thanksgiving that I had other stereotypes to deal with. That night, we'd worked our scheduled two hours and had relaxed, waiting for count to clear. Someone wondered out loud what they'd have for Thanksgiving dinner, and the men decided they'd have turkey, dressing, mashed potatoes, and pumpkin pie.

Then Mr. Harris rubbed his developing pot belly, smiled, and said to nobody in particular, "They used to have a *nice* Thanksgiving here. They'd decorate the chow hall with pretty paper things, little Pilgrims and turkeys and things, and some years they had paper streamers hanging up there. It was all pretty when we walked in the chow hall." The other men stopped talking. "We had turkey and dressing and mashed potatoes—and those potatoes was *real*, too—and green beans. It was really nice. You could go back in the chow line for as many times as you wanted to. But the best part was they had two kinds of pies. They had apple *and* pumpkin, and you could have some of both kinds if you wanted to. Oh, it was *nice!*" Then he frowned and said, "Now, there's no decorations, you can't eat as much as you want to, the potatoes ain't real, and they just have pumpkin pie. Oh, it's a change from the usual, now, but they don't fix it up nice like they used to." He shook his head. "Naaaaw, they brought all that religion into it and messed everything up."

I assumed he meant that somebody objected to the decorations and celebration of the holiday on the basis of separation of church and state. It was past time for count to clear, so I didn't want to start a debate right then. I decided to wait and discuss separation of church and state later on when we studied the Constitution in the Thursday lectures.

In my car that night, I checked my mental to-do list for the dishes I'd take to Thanksgiving dinner at my sister-in-law's house, and then my thoughts drifted to Mr. Harris's monologue. It had surprised me. I knew he had strong opinions and voiced them, so I wasn't surprised he'd raised the issue. His reaction to the food hadn't surprised me either—Mr. Harris would tell you he liked to eat. I'd been surprised by his reaction to the decorations. I'd had no idea that people in prison appreciated—or even noticed—things like paper streamers and little paper turkeys and

Pilgrims. My surprise made me ashamed of the many ways I'd defined people behind bars as different from me...without a shred of evidence to support the definition. Talk about *continuing education*!

# FOUR
## Winter 2002–2003
### December

December brought tutor problems. First, Mr. Murray, a bright but unenthusiastic tutor, quit coming to class. He must have been in the tutoring business for the $23.00-a-month tutors' pay, because in the four months he had the job, he missed exactly half of the classes. I took him off of the callout sheet without giving him a chance to change, because he wasn't there for me to talk to—frustrating.

About the same time, Mr. Wells refused to tutor too-tall Mr. Brandon. He said, "Don't ask me to, because I won't! I'm fed up with him and his laziness. I can work with just about anybody, but him and me just don't get along. He's not even trying!"

I started to tell Mr. Wells that if he could work with only selected students, I didn't need him, but I remembered we were already short a tutor and said, "OK, I'll give you somebody else to work with, but this is a one-time deal. I can't afford to have picky tutors."

He muttered, "I understand," and stomped off.

We hired Mr. Ingalls, a fresh-faced young man with light-brown hair, to replace Mr. Murray, and he worked well with Mr. Brandon. Things looked good for a couple of weeks...until Mr. Ingalls told me that Mr. Lee, the tutor with the many tattoos, was on lockup. "They locked him up because one of the officers said Lee had done a tattoo for me, but we're appealing that. I'm hoping he'll get out pretty quick."

At the next class, Mr. Ingalls bounced into the room, smiling. "The doc looked at my tattoo and said it was an old one, so Lee should be getting off lockup soon."

At the class after that, Mr. Ingalls said Mr. Lee had been transferred to a different facility, and by the following class, they'd also transferred Mr. Ingalls. I went back to square one with Mr. Brandon.

Mr. Fuller had let us have three tutors, and we'd barely managed with that number. Now we had only one, and I was desperate. That's when I remembered Mr. Meyer. I'd met him during my orientation. He had a long, bushy beard, shoulder-length salt-and-pepper hair, and a big smile. He usually wore the smile, but you never knew what hairstyle he'd have. He might look the way he had when we'd met, he might be clean-shaven with a shaved head, he might have any combination of those looks, or he might have a hair or beard length that fell somewhere between the two. He was forty-nine years old, at least six feet tall, and burley.

He'd walked toward Mr. Fuller and me in the hall and said, "Oh, you must be the new teacher. If you need any help, just let me know, and I'll come and give you a hand. I've been teaching for a long time, and I know what I'm doing."

I'd said, "Thanks, I'll keep that in mind."

After he'd walked by, Mr. Fuller had said, "I'd think twice about hiring him, if I were you. He's an intelligent man, but Ms. Gelzer used him as a tutor and had to let him go. The last straw came when he argued with her in class about something she'd said…and not for the first time. She was right, but he insisted that she didn't know what she was talking about. He's still helping in Ms. Treanor's math class, and that seems to be working out all right. He's available, but you'll have to use your own judgment about what you want to do."

I hadn't needed another tutor then and had forgotten about him, but suddenly, Mr. Meyer sounded pretty good. I went to school early to talk to Mr. Fuller about my tutor issues. He said he'd try to get new tutors for us and suggested I talk to Ms. Treanor before I made up my mind about Mr. Meyer. He added, "One thing in his favor is that he's available immediately."

Ms. Treanor hadn't left for the day, and I asked her about Mr. Meyer. She said, "He's smart and works hard. I don't have a problem with him as long as I can keep him from getting too pushy."

Mr. Meyer sounded OK, so I asked Mr. Fuller to send him to our room for the next class. He did and also hired Mr. Watkins to fill the other slot.

Mr. Watkins, a soft-spoken, fifty-year-old man with a warm, comforting smile, had a light complexion, sparse mustache, shaved head, and slightly stooped shoulders. He told me, "I've just transferred here. I requested the transfer so I could get a job in SUI to help me maintain my skills as a cabinet maker. I want you to understand that I'll only be with you until I get the job."

Mr. Fuller had told me Mr. Watkins had years of tutoring experience. He also was simultaneously at ease and enthusiastic—too good to turn away. I told him we had seventeen students working on seventeen different assignments and I'd appreciate any amount of time he could give us.

After class that day, I told Mr. Wells how happy I was over the new tutor. Mr. Wells said, "Yeah, you *know* he was one of the ones got caught up in that Rodney Stokes thing, don't you?"

"I'm not sure what you mean."

"Oh yeah, you remember who Rodney Stokes was, that dude kilt his ex-girlfriend and shot himself when he was out on work release?"

I vaguely remembered reading about it in the paper and seeing it on TV when it had happened, and after I got home that night, I did a little research to refresh my memory. Before June 1993, if people who were sentenced to life in prison in Maryland followed the prison rules, got a prison job, and otherwise convinced the parole board they'd reformed, they could be released on parole after they'd served at least fifteen years of the sentence, minus good time. Their release was by no means automatic after that, but they were eligible for consideration for release from then on. The judges were aware of that when they imposed life sentences instead of life without parole.

It was common for a judge at a sentencing hearing to assume an early release when handing down a life sentence, as the judge had at Mr. Kingsley's hearing, when he'd said, "You will still be a young man when you get out," and gone on to tell Mr. Kingsley to come out of prison ready to go on with his life, not angry and bitter.

Then in June 1993, Rodney Stokes, a lifer in a work-release program, fatally shot his former girlfriend and killed himself. Maryland's governor, Parris Glendening, had ordered the other 134 lifers in work-release programs to go back to maximum-security prisons. He ultimately said that "life means life" and that he'd parole lifers only if they were elderly or dying. That had effectively resentenced the 134 men to life without parole.

In the case of one of my students, Mr. Bryant, the judge had refused to accept a plea bargain of a twenty-five-year mandatory sentence. The judge had said that would be too much time for Mr. Bryant to serve. Instead, the judge had issued a life sentence so that, with good behavior, Mr. Bryant could be paroled earlier. When we started our class in 2002, Mr. Bryant had been in prison for twenty-six years.

Mr. Wells had gone on to tell me about Mr. Watkins' case. "Yeah, Brother Watkins got caught up in it. He'd been on work release for several years, had a fiancée and a baby on the way, and everything, and they sent him back up into maximum security. That's the way they did everybody. Said they'd review each case to decide who could go back out, but that never happened."

Later, Mr. Watkins told me he'd been on work release for six years and for five years had been on family-leave status, which meant he could be away from the facility for forty-eight hours on weekends. He had met his fiancée on his work-release job in a furniture-making shop, and he wanted to go back there to work. Even after all those years, they wanted him back.

He and his fiancée had planned to marry as soon as he got out, and he had everything to look forward to…every reason to continue the new life he'd begun. Then Rodney Stokes and Governor Glendening had taken all of that away.

Mr. Watkins's fiancée and son remained a big part of his life. I marveled that, fourteen years after being snatched from the brink of a normal, productive life, Mr. Watkins could endure and could remain a warm, courageous human being. I knew I'd never be able to understand how he did it.

\* \* \*

I assumed we'd resolved our tutoring issues, but I'd underestimated Mr. Meyer. He cared a lot about the students he tutored, and Ms. Treanor was right about his intelligence, but the man did want to control the class. At least he confined most of his demonstrations of intellectual superiority to the days I did the Thursday lectures.

I tried to teach the lecture material on a level everyone in the room could understand, and if I said something like, "The planets are held in orbit around the sun by the sun's gravity, just like we're held on the earth by the earth's gravity," he might boom out, "I see what you're trying to say, but I definitely wouldn't stop there. What about Kepler's Laws? Those are vital concepts that you're overlooking."

I'd clench my teeth and brush off his comment with, "Well, I don't think the GED goes into that kind of detail." He was a distraction, but I thought I had a remedy. The students who'd passed the TABE—Mr. Adams-Bey, Mr. Hannah-Bey, and Mr. Nichols—had nearly mastered all of the GED subjects except math. Also, Mr. Kingsley still came to class to keep his math skills sharp until he could take the GED. They needed someone to work with them as a group, but I couldn't do it. I had thirteen other students who needed my attention. Besides, the group would've created too much noise in the classroom.

Both to meet the four student's needs and to get Mr. Meyer out of my classroom, I sent them all down the hall to work in a storage room. Mr. Fuller had said we could use it because the officer locked all the classrooms except ours at the end of the regular school day. The storage room was littered with a scarred table, broken chairs and desks, old file cabinets, and boxes of outdated books. A black chalkboard hung on the wall. It wasn't pretty, but it had the essentials.

The move didn't solve my problem with Mr. Meyer, however. I'd told the math students they had to check in with me and give me their homework before they went to the storage room and that they had to come to the Thursday lectures. It hadn't occurred to me that Mr. Meyer would come, too, but come he did, and his interruptions escalated. One Thursday, I realized that as soon as he walked in the door, I became nervous, anticipating his interruptions. I had to do something to change that.

At the end of the day, when Mr. Meyer brought the math group's books and other materials to the file cabinet, I said, "Mr. Meyer, you and I need to talk. There can be only one teacher in the classroom, and I'm it. You're the tutor, and I don't appreciate being blindsided when I'm teaching. If I make a mistake, tell me after class, and we'll work through it. If I'm wrong, I'll tell the men the next time we meet, but I'm not getting into a debate with you in front of the other men."

Mr. Meyer said he saw my point, and then he came to only one more Thursday lecture. He told me he'd stopped coming because he didn't think he could hold his tongue any longer. I appreciated that, told him so, and relaxed.

Mr. Fuller solved the rest of our tutor problems when he hired Mr. Carson, a thirty-three-year-old Army veteran, stocky, with a medium complexion and a baby face. Mr. Carson had a large tattoo of his first initial on his muscular arm and a small gold cross around his neck. He was a math whiz and also worked well with Mr. Brandon...peaceful routine restored.

\* \* \*

Shortly before the holiday break, I walked into the school hallway, saw that head with the white washrag on top, and went squealing after it. "Mr. Adams-Bey, you're back! This is great! Oh, I'm so glad to see you; I was afraid they wouldn't let you back in!"

With a shy, sweet smile that surely made the angels sing, he said, "Yeah, I'm back," walked into the classroom, and got to work.

That felt like an early Christmas present, and another one arrived when we got the scores from the pre-GED test that Mr. Nichols and Mr. Taylor-El had taken earlier that month. They'd passed everything but math, pulling their scores up in some subjects from below a middle-school level. All of us shared the pride that those men felt, and the news let us end 2002 in the enthusiasm of success.

I wanted to give the class an end-of-year reward—also something to celebrate the holiday season—but I faced the no-gift dilemma again. One day, Mr. Lowery boomed out, "Ms. Morrow, it used to be our teacher, she would bring us some Christmas about this time of the year...some little candies or something. You gonna do that?"

"I don't know, Mr. Lowery. The officers at the metal detector won't let me just walk in here with food. I'll see what I can work out."

I asked Mr. Fuller, "Could I get permission to bring in a sealed bag of wrapped candies to pass out to the men at the class before the break?"

"I don't know about that, but I'll get in touch with the warden and find out for you."

He had the answer the next week. "The warden said he can't let us do that because then we'd want to bring stuff in for every occasion."

I thought a minute and said, "Well, what if I bring the men a couple of colorful pencils and pens and a little paper-bound notepad?" (Spiral notepads were banned because of the wire.)

He smiled. "Sounds like school supplies to me!"

I stuck the items I'd listed for Mr. Fuller, plus some lined paper, into colored paper folders—the kind with two pockets inside and metal prongs to hold notebook paper. I gave the tutors a better grade of pencils and pens and a larger notepad; we all knew it was their due. I brought the twenty folders to the last class before the two-week holiday break, and the officers who searched my book bag didn't question them.

Just before time for class to end, I said, "I brought you all some school supplies to use over the holiday break," and handed out the folders, accompanied by a chorus of, "Thanks for the present, Ms. Morrow."

"Wow, Ms. Morrow, I haven't seen a click-pen in a long time. This is great!"

"This is the first Christmas gift I've had in twenty-two (twenty-eight) (thirty-five) years. This sure is nice."

"Ms. Morrow, I can't tell you what this means to me. I hope you and your husband have a good Christmas."

And more of the same. I gave them school supplies; they gave me joyful gratitude that filled my heart.

Actually, they gave me a lot more than that. Back at home, in the usual last-minute rush of preparations for Christmas dinner for twenty-plus at our house, I thought about what the men were experiencing and how grateful they were for the smallest kindness. The thoughts made me feel simultaneously ashamed of our overly indulgent gift-giving and grateful for the freedom to give and receive.

After Christmas dinner, I unwrapped the last gift in my mound of packages, sat back, and appreciated the blessing of family, the joy of celebrating together, and the long tradition of Christmas dinners at our house—where we could go back for more food as many times as we wanted to. Suddenly, it didn't matter that the orange-and-yellow-plaid, frog-bedecked dish towels my cousin gave us were totally tacky and went with nothing in our kitchen. I cherished the love they expressed...grateful to the men who'd taught me to appreciate it.

\* \* \*

## January

The new year got off to a wonderful start when Mr. Fuller told me that Mr. Kingsley had passed the GED. Mr. Kingsley stayed at school that day and soaked up our excitement and congratulations. From that day on, he popped into class occasionally to say "hi" and then rushed to get back to his cell before count started, but he didn't mention graduation.

The other men worked hard—most of the time—and I looked forward to and enjoyed Tuesday and Thursday nights...except for seeing Mr. Perkins. He had a broad, flat face, a heavyset body, and cornrows that ended in braids and twisted the length of his short neck and onto the neck of his white T-shirt. He wore baggy, gray sweatpants, and he grabbed at his crotch a lot when he talked to me. I ignored the grabbing, telling myself he must have some sort of itch. Much of the time, I had to force a smile during our conversations. The man got on my nerves, and I couldn't joke him away or tune him out. It didn't help a bit to remind myself that he was no less a child of God than I.

When Mr. Perkins talked to me, he pattered and laughed. If somebody joined us, say in the staff room, Mr. Perkins still pattered. He didn't stop his patter to acknowledge anything anyone else said but incorporated our comments into his.

It went something like this, "Heh-heh-heh. Yeah, Ms. Morrow got on a new dress tonight. Ms. Morrow went shopping. Heh-heh-heh. She went shopping and bought out the store. Her husband say, 'You sure did do a lot of shopping.' Heh-heh-heh. Yeah, Ms. Morrow got a pretty new dress. Whooo! Ms. Morrow spent a lot of money on that dress. Heh-heh-heh."

"I went shopping, but this is the only thing I bought. It wasn't expensive."

"Heh-heh-heh. Ms. Morrow say it wasn't expensive, she say she only bought one dress. I know Ms. Morrow bought more than one. Heh-heh-heh. Ms. Morrow bought more than one, yeah, I know she did. Heh-heh-heh. Something that pretty got to be expensive. I know that's right. Heh-heh-heh." And on and on and on.

In the classroom, he usually pattered about math. Mr. Perkins had mastered all of the GED tests except writing, which he refused to deal with, and math, which eluded him. He tried; goodness knows he tried, but he insisted on doing things his own way, especially long division. Like the night I called him to my desk, smiled, and said, "Mr. Perkins, when you corrected these problems, you missed a few. Work this first one for me and let me see how you got the answer."

"What! No, no, no! I didn't miss no few. Heh-heh-heh. You know I didn't miss no few. Are you sure you checked those right? Heh-heh-heh. Which ones do you think I missed? Those are *all* right. I know those're right. Heh-heh-heh. Did you work out those answers yourself, or did you look in the back of your book to get those answers? Heh-heh-heh. You better look in the back of your book. You better..."

Straining to keep my smile, I said, "Mr. Perkins, sit down here and show me what you did."

"Heh-heh-heh. Ms. Morrow say, 'Sit down here and show me what you did.' Heh-heh-heh. She say those answers ain't right. I know those answers is right. Ms. Morrow you better go on and put that gold star on my paper right now. Heh-heh-heh. You better…"

I dropped the smile. "Mr. Perkins, how did you get these numbers?"

"OK, this is what I did…." And he'd sit down and show me his method and how it worked on that particular problem. I barely could follow his thought process.

"Mr. Perkins, that won't work. You can't get the right answer if you do it like that."

"Heh-heh-heh. Ms. Morrow say, 'That won't work.' Yes, it do, Ms. Morrow. It maybe don't work for you, but it works for me. Heh-heh-heh. That's my way. It's the way I do it. Ms. Morrow say…."

By that time, my teeth ached with a need to grind, and my smile had long since turned into a grimace. "We'll have to change the way you do it. If you keep doing it this way, you'll keep getting the wrong answers. It's math, Mr. Perkins. It's a science. You can't mess with it. Let's work the problem together."

He'd patter and heh-heh-heh at me and then suddenly become serious and pleasant to work with. Often he'd forget what he'd learned after a few days had passed, but at least he tried.

When he didn't patter, the times he was calm and serious, he was a delight, and we had an easy connection then. It made me sad that this happened so infrequently, and I often hoped my lavender fumes would waft his way.

He'd refused to work with the tutors I assigned to him until Mr. Watkins joined us. They made a good team, mostly because Mr. Watkins had the patience to ride the wave of patter until Mr. Perkins was ready to come ashore and get to work.

I, on the other hand, let Mr. Perkins down. He'd asked me for books to improve his memory, and I brought one in. I intended to bring more but didn't, afraid I'd create more opportunities for patter. Also, I didn't have the education or skill necessary to figure out how to help him with that math. It wasn't much consolation that Ms. Treanor also had students who quickly forgot what they learned. I wanted to give Mr. Perkins a key to the math mystery. The standard one didn't fit, and it was the only one I had. And I failed him a third way. He made every effort to be friends, and most of the time I couldn't reciprocate. Instead, I'd anticipate the onslaught of patter and steel myself against it and him.

But I did give him stars. When he had trouble with math problems, he filled the pages with erasures and smudged changes until he got the problems right. In one class, I returned a paper to him he'd needed more tries than usual to correct. It had a blue star on it from the first time he'd handed it in. He said, "Where's my gold star?" He didn't laugh.

I looked at the smudged paper. "You want a gold star *now*?"

"Of course! Why else would I be doing all this work?"

I could think of other reasons but also thought, "If that's what keeps him motivated, then it's gold stars he'll get," and I put one on his paper.

He started waiting for me after class, to walk with me down the Flats. Some days he left the patter behind, and I enjoyed his company. Other days, he didn't.

One day in mid-January, we walked down the Flats, weaving our way through milk cartons, banana peels, and other garbage that sometimes littered the floor at the end of the day, thrown from the cells by some of the men. I didn't watch where I stepped. Instead, I focused on Mr. Perkins, trying to decipher his patter, and my foot landed on a greasy bone from a fried chicken leg. My foot propelled the bone down the sealed concrete floor, and I rode it like a skateboard. It was ride or crash. My ride lasted only a few seconds, and I was fine, but Mr. Perkins became frantic. He scooted sideways beside me with one arm pumping up and down in the air in front of me and the other in the air behind. He couldn't decide whether to grab me or not.

When I stopped, he said, "You OK? Whew!" and without waiting for my answer, he picked up his patter where he'd left off.

The patter days outnumbered the non-patter days, and toward the end of the month, I started avoiding Mr. Perkins after class...subtly, I thought. But then one day he came to my desk and said in a low voice, "You've quit walking out with me, and it's hurt my feelings."

"I'm so sorry, Mr. Perkins. You know I didn't mean to hurt your feelings." I'd told him the truth, but I couldn't give him any more than that. I cared about him. I tried to help him. I just couldn't take his heh-heh-hehs and the patter that went with them.

\* \* \*

## February

In late February, Mr. Fuller called me into his office, shut the door, and said, "Ms. Treanor's not going to teach the ABE (adult basic education) class any more, and I have no one else to teach it. I wondered if you'd mind taking those students into your class."

That was the class Mr. Fuller had set up to accommodate the men with low reading skills when I'd started teaching. I said, "I'd be happy to."

Mr. Fuller smiled.

A week later, I stood at my file cabinet before class, looked up, and saw a man in the doorway. He was forty-two years old, five feet nine, and wore his hair clipped short. His arms stretched his T-shirt sleeves, and his neck muscles flanged down to his shoulders. He looked like a professional linebacker. He also had a big smile with shiny gold teeth among his bright white ones.

He waited for me to speak first. "Did you want to see me?"

He replied in a deep, soft voice, "I think so. You're Ms. Morrow, aren't you?"

"Yes, I am. Come on in."

He stepped just over the threshold. "My name's Ronald Edwards. I've been in the reading class, but they're closing that down, and they told me to come to your class. Before I do, I want to see if it's all right with you. Did they tell you I was coming today?"

"No, they didn't."

"Then I need to let you know I don't read so good. I was in special-ed classes when I was in school, but it didn't help a whole lot, and I didn't know if you'd want me in your GED class. I work in SUI, but, you know, it's about not reading so good, and all."

"Well, of course we want you in the class. Everybody has to start somewhere. In our class, the men are all in different places with their work, so you'll fit in just fine."

He came to class that day, and he missed only one class after that. A Mr. Foster also arrived that day, and the other three men from the ABE class came over the next two weeks.

They presented a challenge. I didn't want to leave them out of the book-borrowing program but knew they'd have trouble reading the books. I asked them to tell me about their interests anyway and periodically brought magazines in for them: car repair for Mr. Edwards, sports for Mr. Foster and Mr. Brandon, and street rods for Mr. Chadwick. I told them to read as much as they could and to get cues from the pictures.

When the ABE students were finished with the magazines, the other men could borrow one from my desk after class and take it to their cells. The magazines made a huge hit, and the former ABE students were delighted—and a bit smug—over getting to read them first.

I couldn't meet Mr. Norman's interests with magazines, though. He had the highest reading level of the five men, and he told me, "I'm taking a correspondence course to be a Christian minister, and I'd like religious, spiritual things to read."

I asked Mr. Fuller, "If the men specifically request religious materials, would it be OK for me to bring them for reading assignments?"

"If they ask for them, then I'm all for you bringing them in...anything that will get them to read outside of class." Mr. Norman's materials didn't have the circulation of the magazines, but he wasn't the only one who read them, either.

\* \* \*

Soon after the new men joined us, Mr. Carson, the man who tutored too-tall Mr. Brandon, came in the staff room and said, "Ms. Morrow, I wanted to let you know I've gotten a job in SUI. It'll pay me a lot more than tutoring, so I didn't think I could turn it down."

In my mind I screamed, "No, no, no!" But aloud, I said, "Of course you need to take that job. I understand completely."

"Wait, I'm not finished with what I was saying. I'd like to come here as a volunteer tutor, if you think you can arrange that."

I replied with a big smile, "No question. I don't think Mr. Fuller will have a problem with it."

Mr. Fuller had to approve the volunteer assignment for Mr. Carson's name to stay on the callout sheet, and thank goodness he did.

\* \* \*

At the end of the month, Mr. Kingsley's diploma arrived, and Mr. Fuller let me give him a pre-graduation photocopy of it. Mr. Kingsley's smile nearly shot into his ears when I handed him the paper. He walked around the back of the room looking at it. "Yes! Yes, sir! Yes, this is it! Yes!" The rest of us grinned along with him.

The only sad note that February was that Mr. Collins, who'd lost so much weight, came to class less and less often. He looked thinner and weaker each time he came.

# FIVE
## Spring 2003
March

In early March, Ms. Treanor and I had a conversation about Mr. Chadwick, who'd been in her ABE class. Mr. Chadwick could have been on a Chippendale calendar—one of the rare men who made prison clothes look good. He was thirty-six, five feet ten inches tall, and obviously spent just enough time in the weight room. He had a neatly trimmed mustache that hinted at a Fu Manchu and framed a boyish grin…not a grin that said, "I'm still a child and vulnerable," but one that said, "I'm all grown up, but I remember how to play."

The day of my conversation with Ms. Treanor, she was in the staff room when I arrived. She said, "How are you doing with Mr. Chadwick in your class?"

"Fine. He's moving a little slow, but he's doing his work. If he'd try harder, he'd make more progress."

"No, I mean doesn't he frighten you somewhat? He's one of the reasons I cancelled that reading class. I don't know what his crime was, but he scares me."

I'm sure I looked confused. "No, he doesn't frighten me at all."

She said, "Well, I don't know, but I don't think it's just me," and left for the day.

I mulled over my experiences with Mr. Chadwick, looking for something I'd missed, but nothing about him frightened me.

Finally, I thought, *Maybe he emits too much testosterone for Ms. Treanor's comfort level.*

\* \* \*

Later in the month, we got the results from a pre-GED test that three of the advanced students had taken. Mr. Nichols had passed everything, and Mr. Hannah-Bey and Mr. Taylor-El had passed everything but math.

Mr. Adams-Bey, with his white washrag, had said, "I'm not taking the test this time. I'm afraid I forgot too much when I was on whatchcallit lockup." I'd thought he knew enough to pass, but confidence was a necessary element, so I'd let him slide.

Mr. Taylor-El, who still half-danced to my desk to chat once or twice during class, shuffled in the day we got his grades from the pretest. He sagged into the chair next to me and said softly, "Let me ask you something. I know there's some people can't learn much of anything, but are there other people who, you know, can learn some things but can't learn other things, something like maybe, you know, math or something? Like maybe is it something wrong with their brains?"

I said, "OK, first of all, your brain is fine. Look at the scores on your latest pre-GED tests, *including* the ones in math, and look where you were when you started this class. If there was something wrong with your brain, you couldn't have learned as much as you have in this short time. Not only that, you got high scores in reading and writing and a perfect score on your essay. Do you know how few people do that? If something was the matter with your brain, those scores would've been impossible." Maybe I exaggerated, but I thought he needed the exaggeration.

He still drooped. "Yeah, I see what you're saying."

I hadn't gotten through to him. "What are you good at, Mr. Taylor-El?"

"Well, I draws, and I writes. You seen my stuff."

"Exactly, and that's what's known as right-brain dominance." I wasn't sure I'd picked the correct side but didn't think that mattered just then. "People usually have one side of the brain that's stronger than the other side. The side that lets us draw and write and do other creative things well is not the same side that lets us do math well. If one side is exceptionally strong, the other side only seems weak in comparison. Your strong, dominant right side gives you your creative abilities, but that doesn't mean anything's wrong with your left side."

"What did you say that was called again?"

"Right-brain dominance."

"That must be what I got! OK, then I'll keep on trying, because I gots to get this GED, and you know why."

* * *

## April

In 2003, April truly was the cruelest month. It started with Mr. Chadwick, who'd frightened Mrs. Treanor. When we worked at my desk, he'd focus on the work for only a few minutes at a time, then look up and scan the area around us, as he did during any conversation. He'd continue to talk but pan the room with his eyes, turning his head quickly from one side to the other. Then he'd refocus on me or his work. He looked like a man who didn't need to worry about his personal safety, but I guess he didn't feel that way.

One moonless night in early April, Mr. Chadwick sat next to me, across the room from the windows, and we had our heads together, going over his work. During a safety scan, he suddenly stopped talking. He had the look of wonder that a child gets watching a butterfly emerge from its cocoon. He pointed to the windows. "Look, Ms. Morrow. Look!"

I couldn't see anything in the darkness outside to cause his reaction, but he didn't give me time to say so. He turned to Mr. Lowery, sitting close by, and said, "Eddie, look out the window!"

Mr. Lowery looked out and then turned back, obviously as puzzled as I was. Mr. Chadwick said to him, "The *lights*, look at the lights!"

"That's just headlights from the cars out on the road, man."

Still with wonder, Mr. Chadwick replied, "Yeah, I know." Then his face lost expression, and he lowered his head and stared at the floor. A few seconds later, he looked at me and whispered, "Ms. Morrow, I been in here a long time." He stood slowly and went back to his desk, shaking his head, schoolwork behind him for the night.

On my drive home, I tried to imagine life in a cell with no window and wondered what made us feel we needed to treat people that way.

* * *

The next blow to my heart came when Mr. Collins, who'd lost even more weight, returned from a long stretch of absences. He slumped into the staff room before class and showed me a piece of notebook paper with a few slanted lines of words scrawled across it in pencil—far from his former precise handwriting. He paced in front of me, speaking much faster than usual and running his words together. "Ms. Morrow, look here. I tried to write you that essay, but I couldn't do it. I couldn't think of nothing to say. I can't never think of nothing to say now. My mind's messed up."

His thoughts seemed to ricochet inside his head, and he started ranting. He talked about how he couldn't think right "since what happened, since I got sick," about having to testify and about how he tried to put it out of his mind, but it wouldn't "turn me aloose," about how they were still after him, and about how nobody could help him.

He said more. The words came out in a torrent—too fast and too tumultuous for me to make sense of them. I couldn't distinguish the pieces, let alone know how to fit them together. I didn't know whether he was hallucinating, but I knew he was disturbed beyond my ability to help.

When he finally paused, I said, "Mr. Collins, you've been talking to me for some time. Obviously you have strong feelings about what you've said, so write those feelings down, just however they come out. They don't have to make sense. We'll look at that together. I think you'll see you have a lot to say."

He calmed down some and nodded. "I can try to do that, but I can't come to class today. I can't think straight. I need some rest." I agreed, and he walked off mumbling, "I can't get no rest. I can't never get no rest."

Before our next class, Mr. Meyer, the advanced-math tutor, told me they'd put Mr. Collins in protective custody, which is essentially solitary confinement with a few privileges thrown in.

The following week, Mr. Meyer said, "I talked to an officer who works on the protective custody tier, and he told me Collins is in pretty bad shape. He's constantly hallucinating and screaming."

"You mean to tell me he's in that condition and still in a *cell*? Why haven't they taken him to a *hospital*?"

Mr. Meyer muttered, "This is prison."

My heart broke a little more each time I saw Mr. Collins's empty desk that night, and I tried not to think about the horror of what he was going through. I controlled my thoughts pretty well in class, but when I got in the car to drive home, the thoughts and feelings overpowered me. I felt as though I were between two horses, one tied to my mind, the other tied to my heart, pulling in opposite directions.

My years as a civil rights lawyer had trained me to jump into situations like this and do my best to correct them. My heart and most of my mind screamed, "Do something! Help that man!" The other piece of my mind reminded me that I could either remain a teacher or become an advocate.

Rules from the Maryland Department of Correction and Department of Education forbade us to have any relationship with the men beyond the role of teacher in the classroom. We couldn't write to them, we weren't supposed to talk to them outside of the school, and we certainly weren't supposed to advocate for them.

I had to choose between teaching and advocacy. I'd told the men that on my first day, when Mr. Lowery asked if I were a lawyer, but I hadn't had to confront it as an actual choice, certainly not in a situation that normally would've thrown me into action. I reminded myself that I'd made an important commitment to a room full of men and chose to stick to my role as teacher. I never could decide whether I made the right choice.

After that, I occasionally smelled cigarette smoke on one or two of the men, and on even rarer occasions smelled alcohol on one or two. The prison had banned both cigarettes and alcohol, but I decided that if my role as teacher didn't allow advocacy, then it didn't require policing, either, except as it related to my teaching.

About a week later, Mr. Collins was transferred to another prison. I never knew where they housed him there, but I did know that his treatment at the Cut wasn't unusual. Back when I was a lawyer, I'd pored over data from the National Association on Mental Illness in connection with one of my cases. The data detailed the inhumane treatment of mentally ill inmates. What I saw on paper back then had horrified me, but not nearly so much as the knowledge of what the prison had done to my student.

\* \* \*

## May

May began with another lockdown, and we missed several classes. When we got back to school, Mr. Harris, who'd described the Thanksgiving decorations, came to my desk with a frown on his face. "What does it mean when you see dots in front of your eyes and things are going dim?"

"It *may* mean that you have cataracts or that the lining of your retinas is starting to pull away. Those things happen as we age. What it *definitely* means is that you need to go see the doctor."

At the next class, Mr. Harris said he'd asked for an appointment, but the optometrist didn't come there often, and there was a waiting list for exams. I said, "Did you tell the officers what was happening with your eyes?"

He replied, "Yeah, but they said I'd have to wait my turn."

"Well in the meantime, just be extra careful and try not to hit your eyes or jerk your head around." And to myself I said, "You decided you'd be a teacher. You decided you'd be a teacher. You decided you'd be a teacher."

\* \* \*

Toward the middle of the month, Ms. Treanor, Ms. Gelzer, and I stood in the hall, chatting before class. Mr. Chadwick walked up, leaned in toward Ms. Treanor, and said, "Hey, Pretty Baby," and similar things that I was too stunned to remember. He used a deep, rumbling voice, and the boyish grin became a lascivious smirk. That went beyond sexy, and I had no doubt then why Ms. Treanor had cancelled her class. I suspected that Mr. Chadwick thought he was kidding around with her, but I also suspected that he enjoyed the effect he had.

As I walked down the hall to our room, the disparity between the man I'd believed Mr. Chadwick to be and what I'd just seen made me hope he wouldn't need much help from me that night. I couldn't be sure of my reaction to him one on one—not until I'd had time to find a more comfortable response to the dichotomy.

After class, I sipped black coffee on the drive home and thought about Mr. Chadwick's behavior. Finally, I decided Mr. Chadwick remained the person I'd known all along. I hadn't known him completely, but what I had known hadn't changed. I would react only to the man in my classroom. His leer and words still rankled, but my thoughts gave me a way to accept him as my student.

\* \* \*

Toward the end of May, when Mr. Meyer and I chatted in the staff room, he told me he expected to get out in about a year. He said, "You know what I'm looking forward to doing after I get out?" He smiled in anticipation and said in a dream-filled voice, "I want to cook something for myself and sit down and enjoy it. I don't care whether it's something fancy or just a burger. I'm an *excellent* cook, and I want to cook something *just* the way I like it."

The men didn't have food options in the chow hall. The kitchen cooked one meal, and the men either ate it or didn't eat.

At home that night, I stirred red beans with Louisiana sausage in a pot on the stove, reheated rice in the microwave, toasted garlic bread in the oven, and tore greens for a salad. I tried to imagine going for years without being able to make my own food choices or to prepare food to my taste. From that night on, I felt grateful for the opportunity to fix dinner...even on the nights when the last thing I wanted to do was cook.

# SIX
## Summer 2003
### June

Toward the middle of June, Mr. Watkins got his job in SUI. He'd warned me that he'd leave when the job came through, but it still came as a blow when he said he wouldn't be back. His strength of character and calm presence had meant as much to me as it had to the men.

Mr. Fuller hired a Mr. Hynson to take Mr. Watkins's place. Mr. Hynson was twenty-nine, of medium height, and kept his black hair, mustache, and goatee short, just this side of shaved. Solid-black tattoos decorated his muscular upper arms. Many months after he joined us, he told me his Filipino mother and American father had moved to the United States from the Philippines when he was six months old. His smooth, tan complexion reflected his mother's genes.

In class, Mr. Hynson reminded me of a cat, aloof and alert, watching to decide whether he could approach and be safe…and whether he wanted to. His speech came in machine-gun–rapid staccato, and it may not have helped things that I scrunched up my face and stared hard at him, straining to understand what he said. Both of us settled in to see what would develop.

* * *

Near the end of June, Mr. Fuller called me to his office and said, "If I schedule a class for a couple of hours on the same days you're teaching now, say from twelve-fifteen to two-fifteen, and add a paid planning period, say from two-thirty to three-thirty, would you be interested in taking the class?"

I ignored my New Year's resolution to quit saying *yes* to things automatically. "Sure, I could do that."

Mr. Fuller smiled. "Good. I'll be back in touch when I know something definite."

At his office door, I turned and said, "By the way, what class would I teach?

"I'm thinking about a math lab at the Annex (where he also was the principal) for men who are getting ready to take the GED."

I said, "Oh, OK, that would be great," and tried to appear composed. Not only did he want me to teach men who already knew enough algebra, geometry, and other higher math to pass the pre-GED test, but I'd have to teach at the Annex. People had told me horror stories about the place almost since I'd started at the Cut. Mr. Fuller had said the state housed men with sentences of life without parole over there, and other teachers had told me that trying to keep order in the classrooms was a nightmare, that the students were loud and disrespectful. Also, the facility went on lockdown a lot because of rival gang violence. I wouldn't go back on my word to Mr. Fuller, but I hoped that I wouldn't have to keep it.

That same day, Mr. Kingsley stopped by before class, as he'd done off and on since he passed the GED. I never asked how he managed to get a pass to do that. He stood in front of my desk, on the same spot where he'd announced, "Stump can't do no algebra," and said, "You remember you told us that if we graduated you'd give us a portfolio?"

I nodded.

"Is that still true?"

"Yes."

"Well, I don't want just any portfolio; I want that one." He pointed to the one I brought to school with me—a coppery, plastic folder with places for a writing pad and pen on the right and plastic dividers for papers on the left.

I squealed, "You're going to the graduation! You're going to go!" My smile almost matched his.

The smiles and banter from the other men said they also recognized the importance of his decision. He needed the affirma-
tion the graduation ceremonies gave…hard to find in prison.

"Did you hear that? Stump's going to the graduation!"

"Stump's gonna walk!"

"Alright now, Stump!"

* * *

# July

Friday, July 11, I went to the Cut but didn't turn right at Center Hall to go to the Flats. Instead, I turned left, walked through
a double gate, crossed a concrete corridor, and went down a narrow hall to a door where an officer checked my ID. Then I
walked into the chapel and sat with the other teachers and staff on
the second pew from the front. Darien "Stump" Kingsley was
graduating, and nothing short of a major heart attack could have
kept me away.

That was the first time I'd seen the chapel, a large room that
had as airy a feel as a cream-colored room with a concrete floor
could have. High, barred windows filled both of the side walls,
and the sunlight that streamed through them brought relief to the
grimness. Ms. Treanor and her committee of prisoners had
painted banners with words of congratulations and the class
motto, "Moving in the Right Direction," and had taped them
around the walls. Three sections of pews faced the podium in the
front of the room. Faculty, staff, and guests sat in the section on
the left; members of the band, tutors, and school office clerks—
the only nongraduating prisoners allowed to attend—sat on the
far right. The center section remained empty, awaiting the graduates.

Ms. Gelzer, in charge of the ceremony, punched the play but-
ton on the cassette player, and Mr. Kingsley and the fifteen graduates from the regular day school marched in to a tinny "Pomp
and Circumstance."

I suspected that the graduates' caps and gowns once had been
maroon, but they'd faded to a medium rose…one size fits all. The
men six feet tall or over wore gowns that came well above their

knees and showed a good-sized chunk of their prison uniforms underneath. Mr. Kingsley's gown hung around his ankles. Not one hem fell straight. The tarnished gold tassels hung on all sides of the rose-colored mortarboards. The graduates marched in with no prison slump in their shoulders. Each man carried himself as though he were royalty.

The ceremony surprised me by being just like every other graduation ceremony I'd attended—except there were no balloons, gifts, or flowers; only the official prison photographer could have a camera; and the ages of the graduates ranged from twenty to fifty-six. Officials from the school system gave congratulatory speeches; the inmate band performed two numbers; the valedictorian spoke; the keynote speaker gave an upward-and-onward oration that lasted too long; the graduates went to the front when their names were called, received their diplomas, and shook hands with the officials; and people in the audience applauded and cried.

Earlier in the week, I'd told Mr. Fuller I planned to give a portfolio to Mr. Kingsley after the ceremony, and he'd said, "After all that man has been through to get this diploma, I don't see any reason for you not to give it to him. After all, he is your first SUI program graduate, and we're authorized to give out awards." Mr. Fuller *hadn't* said he would call me to the dais to present the award.

The tutors from our class formed a cheering section for Mr. Kingsley, and they outdid themselves when I asked him to join me on the dais to receive the coppery plastic portfolio. Mr. Kingsley, shy and subdued, with no hint of coiled-spring energy, stood a little distance from me while I made the presentation. Like the Cheshire Cat, only the smile remained.

Each graduate could have two approved guests at the ceremony, but only a few men had anyone there. Mr. Kingsley's parents had driven for well over an hour to attend, and after the prison photographer took the group graduation picture, Mr. Kingsley called me over to meet them. His father wore a suit with a shirt and tie. His mother wore a suit with a silk blouse and pumps with two-inch heels. They were trim and about Mr. Kingsley's height. When I walked over, the elder Mr. Kingsley grabbed me and pinned my arms in a big bear hug. He let me go, and Mrs. Kingsley followed suit. I didn't know whether to laugh or cry. We all did both.

* * *

On July 24, Mr. Fuller stayed late to tell me he'd decided to have the math lab at the Annex. I'd become rather self-satisfied at the Cut, thinking I had that *we're all one* thing pretty well mastered. But when a couple of teachers told me more about the inmates at the Annex, I didn't think it likely I'd be able to see myself in their eyes—surely not in the eyes of a man who'd murdered a family of strangers in cold blood.

The fear I'd known early on at the Cut came back, too, except I didn't fear what the men might do to me but rather that they might act out, that I wouldn't be able to control the class. I tried to think of a reason to give Mr. Fuller for not doing the lab, but nothing short of the truth, which I didn't want to admit, sounded plausible...even to me.

I had a quotation from Eleanor Roosevelt under the plastic protector on my desk top: "You must do the thing you think you cannot do." I repeated those words a lot the day Mr. Fuller gave me the news about the lab...and even more on July 29, the first day I taught it.

High, parallel, hurricane fences, which had coils of razor wire across the tops and bottoms and piled in between, separated the Cut from the Maryland House of Correction Annex. The Annex had opened in 1991, and had long, single-story, brick buildings. The same building entrance and metal detector served both the Cut and the Annex, but once through the metal detector, the differences between the facilities began.

First, I had to wait in the area beyond the metal detector until an officer from the Annex came to escort me to the school. The longest I waited was fifty minutes, but twenty to thirty minutes became the norm. The wait would've bothered me less if I'd had some place to sit. Inside the Annex, officers did their own search of my body and then took all of the things out of my book bag and spread them on a table. Often, no officers were available to do the search, and I had to stand in a hallway and wait again. Also, the teachers and staff were supposed to wear body alarms (black boxes the size of a cigarette pack that we could activate to emit a siren wail and summon officers), but, except for two days early on, the officers had issued all of them before I arrived—a relief because I found them a nuisance to carry around.

Once in class on the first day, I saw clear differences between the SUI class and the math lab. The lab had twenty-five students, many of them young, and about a third of them either white or Hispanic; my desk and chair were newer, although I still faced the sides of the men's heads; the school wing had air conditioning; and the officers locked us inside the classroom.

Also, I recognized some of the men. I'd seen them on TV, men who'd committed such sensational crimes that I'd remembered their faces, including the man who'd murdered the family and one who'd committed a particularly brutal series of rapes and murders. I told myself that the men I recognized were no different from the men at the Cut, that they'd only committed more-serious crimes. Still, I didn't want to get close enough to look into their eyes.

Then it dawned on me that the success I'd had at the Cut hadn't come from any particular skill or knowledge on my part. It had happened because I'd related to the men, person to person, and gained their trust. When I looked at them and said, "You can do this work," they'd believed me. I needed to develop that same level of trust in the math lab.

To start the process, I walked to each man's desk, gave him an assessment test, and forced myself to look into his eyes and smile. Most of the men smiled back and said "thank you." After that, I felt more comfortable.

When my first qualms settled, only one student made me feel uneasy. I'd recognized Mr. Shipman's name from newspaper stories about his crime, but that wasn't what did it. He sat in the far back corner, slouched at his desk—all six-feet-plus of him—with his wavy mop of blond hair just above the chair back and his legs splayed and stretched straight out. The smirk on his face said, "Bring it on." He made a show of ignoring everything I said to do and yelled out inane questions and comments. I responded as briefly as I could at first, then reacted with an "Oh, really now" teacher look, and finally ignored him.

I told everyone to start the assessment test, and Mr. Shipman, with an overstated flourish, moved his desk several feet forward so that its writing arm butted into the writing arm of Mr. Boyd's desk. Mr. Boyd was a quiet young man with cornrows and a serious demeanor. Mr. Shipman made a show of copying from Mr. Boyd's paper, and as the tension level in the room rose, I felt my feared loss of control becoming a reality.

I knew if I gave Mr. Shipman a stage, he'd take the lead role that I claimed as my own, so I walked to his desk and stood close to him with my back to the other students except Mr. Boyd. I said softly, "Mr. Shipman, this is a test. If it's going to mean anything, each person has to do his own work. I want you to move back where you were."

His response boomed, his expression cocky, "But I'm not copying off *him*; he's copying off *me*!" No one behind me made a sound.

"Well, Mr. Shipman, I want you to move back where you were so he can't do that. I need to see what he's capable of doing by himself."

Not a single pencil moved, and Mr. Boyd looked as though he'd like to dissolve. Mr. Shipman stood up slowly, stretched, and made a point of taking his time. I didn't move. Finally, he inched his desk back to the corner where it had been. I thanked him, turned, watched heads snap around to look back at test papers, and walked to my desk. I'd been in my chair about two minutes when Mr. Shipman got up, pushed the buzzer for an officer to let him out, and left. If that was to be the last word, I was happy for him to have it. I never saw him again. The math lab continued peacefully.

* * *

## August

In early August, the great good news came that Mr. Hannah-Bey and Mr. Taylor-El had passed the pre-GED test and could take the GED exam. I called the two men into the staff room before class and gushed out their results. They both reacted with big smiles, but Mr. Hannah-Bey squared his shoulders and held his head up high, while Mr. Taylor-El bent over and wriggled with excitement.

"Really, Ms. Morrow? You're not kidding me, now are you? I thought sure I'd messed up that math again!"

I announced the news to the rest of the class, and we sat in the hot classroom, sweating and grinning. Even the new tutor, Mr. Hynson, who didn't bestow smiles freely, had a grin on his face.

Despite the grin that day, Mr. Hynson still kept his distance from me. He worked well with the men, but he said very little to me beyond a hello when he came into the room and a good-bye when he left…until the day Mr. Taylor-El and some of the other men started talking about the fall leaves I'd brought in the year before.

After a class in mid-August, as we fanned ourselves with notebook paper and waited for count to clear, Mr. Taylor-El bounced into the room and sat by my desk. He said to the other men, "You remember the day Ms. Morrow brought all those leaves to class?" The men laughed, and we bantered back and forth, as we'd done so many times with the leaf story.

Mr. Hynson looked at the rest of us as though we'd lost it. Mr. Taylor-El said, "That's right, Ren wasn't here back then. Tell him what you did, Ms. Morrow."

Mr. Hynson pulled an empty desk close to mine and sat down. I told the story of the leaves, and the men added their comments.

"Yeah, you should have seen it, Ren. We didn't know what was going on!"

When that died down, Mr. Hynson said, "I wish I'd been here to see that. I bet it was beautiful." He paused. "You know what I'd like most from the outside? I'd like to walk across a soft carpet, and I'd like to feel tree bark."

I struggled with it, but I just couldn't do anything about the carpet. After I brought the bark for Mr. Hynson, he relaxed a little around me, and toward the end of August, he came to my desk with a stack of photos in his hand. "Ms. Morrow, can I show you these pictures?"

I said, "Sure," and he sat down, handed me the pictures, one by one, and told me the name and relationship of each family member: mother, half-sister, brother, cousins, and adopted siblings. He smiled the whole time, and I almost heard him purr.

\* \* \*

Mr. Kingsley still stopped in occasionally to chat before class started. At the end of the month, instead of popping in and out, he sat in a desk in the front of the room, well past the time count began. I thought it strange, but by then I didn't ask questions without a need to know.

After I took roll, Mr. Kingsley stood by his desk and said that he and the rest of the class were upset because I hadn't gotten a plaque at the graduation ceremony, as some of the full-time teachers had. After the ceremony, Mr. Hynson had asked me why I hadn't received a plaque, and I'd told him I was a part-time, contract teacher with just one class, had taught at the Cut a short time, and had only one graduate, so I hadn't earned one. It had seemed right to me.

I'd forgotten about the plaque until Mr. Kingsley stood by his desk and said they thought I was the best teacher at the Cut, and if anybody deserved a plaque, I did. He opened a manila envelope and pulled out a beautiful wooden plaque with a dark maroon plastic face, inscribed in gold and bordered with painted gold scrolling. It was one that had been made in the SUI shop. He read the inscription aloud:

---

### Award for Meritorious Service

### Ms. Merle Morrow
SUI Teacher

### In Appreciation for Your Outstanding Service, Dedication, and unselfish Commitment to the Educational Department at the Maryland House of Correction.

---

On the drive home that night, I realized I'd probably cried more during my year and three months at the Cut than in the previous ten years...at least in front of people.

# SEVEN
## Fall 2003
### September

September began with sad news. First, we had a dropout. Mr. Norman, the man who was studying to become a minister, stopped me in the hall and said, "Ms. Morrow, I know I haven't been to class much lately (he'd come only twice since February), but I'm a supervisor out on the compound, and they're working me overtime almost every night. I don't see no signs of it letting up. I'm gonna drop out so somebody else can have my slot."

"I'm sorry, Mr. Norman, but I do appreciate your telling me. If you ever decide you have time to start coming again—and I hope you will—tell one of the other men to let me know, and I'll get your name back on the callout sheet."

"Thank you, ma'am. I'll try to do that, but I think this is best for me to do right now."

I watched him leave the school wing, certain I'd never see him again.

Mr. Perkins delivered the other sad news. He still pattered at me in the staff room before class, but that time he didn't patter. He said, "Ms. Morrow, Henry Harris won't be coming back for a while."

I said, "Oh, no! Don't tell me he's on *lockup*."

"No, no, no, he's not on lockup. You remember he was having trouble with his eyes...seeing dots and all? Well, today at work, he all of a sudden couldn't see *nothing*. He told his supervisor things had gone dark, and the supervisor—he's from the outside—called people he knew and got Henry in to see the doctor over in the infirmary. Doctor said the retinas in both of Henry's eyes had come loose, and they're keeping him in the infirmary. They're probably going to send him to the hospital in Baltimore to see can they fix his eyes."

"Thanks for telling me, Mr. Perkins. I'll keep him in my prayers."

"Yeah, you do that, and I will, too."

We both knew that was all we could do.

* * *

Things improved toward the end of the month. Mr. Taylor-El took the actual GED exam in early September, and we learned he'd passed everything except math. I worried about his reaction to the math score, but when I gave him the news, he said, "You know, I'm not there yet, but I'm closer than I've ever been. You remember that first day you came to our class? I didn't have much hope about passing this thing then, but I thought I'd come and check you out. You told us there wasn't one of us in that room couldn't get our GED or we wouldn't be in there. You remember that? Well, I decided to see what you could do, and now I really believe it's working. I'm going to pass this thing yet, Ms. Morrow!"

His attitude made me happier than his grades had.

Mr. Hannah-Bey, the man who'd told me he'd never go home, had taken the exam, too, and he passed *everything*. When I called him into the staff room and told him, he gave a whoop, threw his hands in the air, and knocked over a big bulletin board that sat on a table beside him. I'm sure he didn't feel his hand hit the board; it did nothing to diminish a smile too broad to measure. I grabbed the board, and we grinned and jabbered at each other. Suddenly, he realized he didn't need to come to class and rushed out of the room to make it to the cell block before count started. He yelled back over his shoulder, "See you later, Ms. Morrow."

"You'd better believe it! I'm going to be there to see you walk up that aisle at graduation."

A big "Yes!" came from the other side of the gate to the school.

* * *

## October

Early in October, Mr. Aloona, the quiet man who'd taught himself to read, did more to convince the class that hard work pays off than I could've done with twenty-six pep talks. He passed the TABE. He'd learned *so* much in such a short time, and his success gave a boost to the men and a wonderful send-off to my vacation.

I'd signed up to spend October 3 through 20 with Habitat for Humanity building houses in Oukasie Township, South Africa—Ciro, my husband, had had a schedule conflict and stayed home. The men had been as excited about the trip as I was. I'd asked Mr. Fuller whether I could get permission to send postcards to the men, and he'd told me to ask the chief of security. Chief had said, "No, I can't let you do that. Those would be gifts." I hadn't taken that to mean I couldn't bring the men school supplies, though.

Our second Sunday in South Africa, we'd gone to an open-air market outside of Johannesburg, and I'd asked the people in our group to keep a lookout for anything that might qualify as a school supply. One of the younger group members had run through the stalls to find me and said he'd found leather bookmarks, and the vendor had enough for the whole SUI class. Perfect!

Each bookmark had an indigenous animal tooled and painted on it: a lion, zebra, rhinoceros, or elephant. Back in class, each man chose the animal that appealed most to him, and I selected one to give to Mr. Harris when he returned from his eye surgery. In the midst of smiles and thank-yous, I heard one of the students say, "Somebody made this in *Africa*, man!"

Many of the men had rarely, if ever, left the city or town where they were born, and some had rarely left their own neighborhoods. I wanted them to vicariously take the trip with me. Besides, the trip had spoken to my mind and heart in a deeper way than any other trip I'd taken. The people in Oukasie lived in tiny, corrugated tin boxes in the broiling African sun, and their children walked up dusty dirt roads to schools that were in no way equipped to prepare them for the national test they had to pass to get a diploma.

I wanted to share all of that with the class and decided to bring in my photo albums from the trip, even though we weren't supposed to take personal photos into the Cut. I mentally tested and discarded several justifications to give to the officers at the entrance to get the albums in and finally decided to define them as social studies materials. That's the spiel I gave at the metal detector, but the officers became too engrossed in the albums to acknowledge my brilliant rationale.

The men and I spent the whole class period talking about the pictures and the political and social conditions in South Africa, as well as the history behind them. I told stories about the graciousness and warmth of the people we worked with in the township, and we discussed the ways that their schools and living conditions differed from ours and why.

For a long time after that, I had a waiting list to read Nelson Mandela's book, *Long Walk to Freedom*. I told the men the book was special to me because I'd bought it at the Apartheid Museum in Johannesburg, and they promised to be careful. When everyone had read the book, it had a well-and-gently-read polish.

At the Annex, I did have to use my social-studies-project argument, because the officers refused to let me take the albums in until I cleared them with the security chief over there. Luckily, I got through my social-studies argument and got the chief's approval without having to say I taught a math lab.

After my first day at the Annex, things had gone smoothly. All of the men worked on GED-level math, and I did more lectures and used the chalkboard more than at the Cut. We didn't talk about much beyond homework and class assignments, so I didn't know how the class would react to the albums. Their reaction was similar to that of the men at the Cut, and we had the best, most relaxed exchange of any we had while I was there.

\* \* \*

Toward the end of the month, Mr. Fuller stopped me when I got to school and, with his brows lowered, said, "Ms. Morrow, I hate to tell you this, but Hannah-Bey already *has* a GED."

"What!"

He shook his head. "I got a call this morning from the people at the department of education, and they said he'd earned a GED in prison twenty-seven years ago. He got a diploma then, and of course there's no way they'll give him another one. I took his name off of the callout sheet, so he won't be coming back to the school."

Mr. Hannah-Bey had earned his GED before they had graduation ceremonies, and the school didn't have records from that far back. When he'd enrolled in our GED class, no one had questioned whether he should be admitted. Because Mr. Fuller had taken Mr. Hannah-Bey's name off of the callout sheet, I had no way to talk to him or say good-bye.

About a week later, Mr. Hannah-Bey broke prison rules to wait for me after class. I walked into Center Hall and heard him call, "Ms. Morrow!" from behind the mesh-covered bars across the way. I walked to the bars, and he said, "Ms. Morrow, I'm so sorry I let you down! I just wanted to wear a cap and gown and feel that tassel swing."

Driving home that night, I struggled with the knowledge that Mr. Fuller was correct—Mr. Hannah-Bey couldn't get a second diploma—and the wish that this sixty-year-old man who'd been in prison for more than twenty-seven years could be rewarded for all of his hard work. I knew there had to be many other men who'd earned a GED but hadn't experienced a graduation ceremony, both older men like Mr. Hannah-Bey and those who'd earned a diploma more recently but had been transferred before graduation day. If Mr. Hannah-Bey were allowed to wear his cap and gown, the other men would want to do the same. My mind acknowledged all of that, yet my heart broke for the big man with the twinkling eyes and soft smile.

* * *

# November

In early November, Mr. Fuller announced that he'd decided to retire. Unless he was having a confidential meeting, Mr. Fuller kept the door from his office to the hallway open and welcomed anyone who came by to chat or to discuss school. The men and staff appreciated his openness and respected him. Everyone felt sad about his leaving.

Past and current students and tutors asked Ms. Gelzer to help them put on a program to express their gratitude to Mr. Fuller, and on a Wednesday morning, we gathered in the chapel to say farewell. A former student who spoke during the open-mic portion of the program had a huge impact on me.

His face barely cleared the top of the lectern, where he stood with much throat clearing and less-than-convincing coughs as he adjusted and readjusted the microphone to his height. Finally, he said in a quivering voice, "I just want to thank Mr. Fuller for the way he treated us...you know, not like we was convicts."

The inmates in the audience erupted with laughter, and with a shy grin, he responded, "Yeah, I know, but you know what I mean. He treats us like we're people." The applause that followed was far louder than the laughter had been.

Afterward, Ms. Gelzer told me the assembly was unusual, not something that the men had done when other people left the school. I drove home after the assembly and thought how blessed I'd been to do my first teaching under Mr. Fuller's guidance. I also realized that the men didn't become *convicts* in their own minds or hearts when they came to prison, and I regretted that Mr. Fuller's attitude toward the men wasn't the norm. The nervous speaker's words played in my mind like a song you can't get rid of: "He treats us like we're people." I vowed to let that music find a permanent place in my mind and heart.

\* \* \*

In late November, Mr. Adams-Bey, who'd abandoned the white washrag, stopped me at the classroom door and said, "I got a friend that works in whatchacallit, SUI, and he wanted me to ask you if you could use a volunteer tutor. He got his whatchacallit

GED and everything, and he's looking for a way to give something back. I said I'd ask you about it."

Maybe I was in shock from the length of Mr. Adams-Bey's speech, but I didn't ask anything about the man. I said, "Sure, give me his name, and I'll put him on the callout sheet"...one impulsive decision I didn't regret.

# EIGHT
## Winter 2003–2004
December

M r. Adams-Bey's friend, Mr. Jones-Bey, arrived the first week in December. Much later, he told me he had an Italian mother and an African-American father, and he looked the truth of his heritage. His skin was a shade darker than Mediterranean olive, and he had the smile that makes Italian men so appealing—a bright, narrow slice of allure and joy. He wore his hair in braids, and his build was slight and wiry. He said he'd lived in New York most of his life, and I asked, "What on earth are you doing in prison down here?"

"Oh, I've been all up and down the East Coast doing mischief. Maryland is just where I got caught. Man, I've taken so much. It's time I gave something back."

I didn't have a chance to get to know him or his work very well before the holiday break, because in early December, the Cut went on lockdown. Gratefully, the lockdown ended in mid-December—right before Mr. Adams-Bey, Mr. Nichols, and Mr. Taylor-El were scheduled to take the GED.

Mr. Meyer said Mr. Taylor-El wasn't ready, but I didn't have the heart to tell Mr. Taylor-El he couldn't try. Despite my heart, his chance to try nearly evaporated the week before the exam, when someone stole his glasses. He couldn't read the study materials or the test, and he said it took at least six months to get glasses at the Cut. At dinner the night he told me, I bemoaned Mr. Taylor-El's rotten luck to Ciro. He said, "I think I have some old glasses around here somewhere he might be able to use. I'll take a look when we finish eating."

We had our coffee, and then Ciro went through his drawers and shelves, finding a few pair of bifocals he'd tucked away when he couldn't use them any more. Mr. Taylor-El didn't need correction for distance vision, but this was no time to be picky. At least Ciro found a range of prescriptions for Mr. Taylor-El to try. For the first time, I was grateful that I'd married a pack rat, and for the gazillionth time, grateful for a husband who cared.

Mr. Taylor-El tried on the glasses at his desk and found a pair that worked for him. When he looked through the top part of the lens, he jerked his head back and said they made him queasy, but he saw that as a source of joke material rather than as a problem and wove around like a comic version of a drunk.

Mr. Taylor-El's experience with the glasses joined in my mind with the plights of Mr. Harris and Mr. Collins. I cringed when I thought of the feelings of helplessness that must go along with a lack of control over your life—not to keep things from going wrong, but to fix them when they inevitably did.

Mr. Adams-Bey, Mr. Nichols, and Mr. Taylor-El took the GED exam, and the tension of waiting for their scores settled on our class. The three men still came to school to work on their math skills, in case they hadn't passed.

* * *

One night toward the end of December, count took an unusually long time to clear. When the officer called, "Count's clear," the men rushed out of the school to make it to chow before the serving lines closed down. By the time I'd put my things away and walked onto the Flats, all of the men had left for the chow hall, and their cells stood empty.

I'd never looked into the cells because that felt like an invasion of privacy, and I sure didn't want to observe the men's toileting habits. But with the men gone, I decided to take a peek. The cells measured eight feet by five feet, and each had a steel toilet in the back corner. In each, a museum-worthy basin was attached high on the back wall, and both fixtures had stains that probably pre-dated my birth. A wooden box for the men's clothes and other things sat on the floor against the wall opposite the toilet, and a legless metal bunk hung from the same wall, the inside edge attached to the wall by hinges and the outside edge by chains that spanned the bed. The mattress on the bed looked to be about an inch thick. The only light, except for wire-enclosed incandescent lights in the corridor, came from a bare bulb in a socket that was surrounded by a wire cage on the ceiling.

The experience of seeing those cells devastated me. I walked on down the Flats and to my car, haunted by the thought that anyone—but especially the men I knew—had to live in such conditions. I wondered again how the men kept their sanity, let alone their sense of humor and kindness of heart.

I drove from the parking lot, teary over the way we treat people in our prisons, but by the time I turned onto I-97, anger had replaced the tears. I wanted to scream at people in the passing cars, "*Tell me exactly what it is about the place I just left that reminds you of a country club!*"

Embroiled in thoughts of the men's living conditions, I forgot to call Ciro to tell him I'd be home late, and when I pulled into our driveway, he ran out of the house and onto the porch. I saw his drawn face and heard the fright in his voice as he said, "What *happened*?" It hit me that he worried on nights I went into the prison. He'd never told me.

The next time I talked to my sister, I said how much Ciro's worry surprised me, expecting she'd be surprised, too. She said, "I don't think you realize how much it worries my family and me, either."

Not one of those worried people ever tried to discourage me from working at the prison—quite the contrary—although all were relieved when I later resigned. That's love.

\* \* \*

My anger at the way the men had to live stayed with me…followed by guilt over having so much when the men had so little.

Ciro's niece and her husband owned a condo in Palmas del Mar, a beach resort near Humacao, Puerto Rico—a spacious townhouse with bedrooms on both floors. They offered to let us use it over the holidays, and my sister, her husband, and their three sons came with us to celebrate Christmas and New Year's Eve, visit Ciro's family, and tour the island. We all looked forward to trading the gray chill of our Maryland winter for the Caribbean breezes and sunshine.

That is, I looked forward to it until I remembered the cells and the guilt kicked in. I couldn't imagine a bigger contrast, and I felt terrible about going to Puerto Rico to enjoy all of that beauty while my students sat in cages.

I'd told the men about our planned trip, and after our last day of class, they all thanked me for their holiday school supplies and wished me a good journey. "You soak up some of that sun down there for us now, Ms. Morrow."

"You enjoy yourself and get you some rest."

Mr. Perkins said, "You and your family have a blessed Christmas."

On the way home that night, Mr. Perkins's words came back to me, and I acknowledged that my family and I *had* been blessed. We'd been given the gifts of each other's company and a beautiful tropical island for Christmas. Guilt only besmirched the blessing. And so I left the winter gloom behind with gratitude for the opportunity and a prayer that someday, my students and tutors also could enjoy such a blessing.

* * *

# January

In Puerto Rico, on a mountain trail in El Yunque National Park, I twisted my ankle. If I'd acted like I had good sense, my ankle probably would've been sore but OK, but *noooo*. On New Year's Eve, I wore high heels to a dance, ignoring the pain, and by the time we sang "*Auld Lang Syne*," I'd sprained my ankle and, in the process, broken a bone in my foot.

I limped around until we got back home on January 2, and Ciro convinced me to go to the emergency room. The doctor said I'd have to wear a hard cast and use crutches for a month, until I got a walking cast. I couldn't hobble from my car to the classroom on crutches, with all of the books and papers I had to carry back and forth, so I missed the first month of school, and the men did, too—no substitute teachers in prison.

Mid-January, the men sent me a card. Mr. Hynson had cut the tab off of a manila file folder, drawn a big, fluffy teddy bear standing on its head on the front, shaded the whole thing with colored pencils, and drawn a border around the edges. Above the teddy bear, he'd lettered "ANY WAY YOU" and below it "LOOK AT IT…" and inside lettered, "YOU'RE A GREAT TEACHER!! GET WELL SOON!!" He'd circulated the card through the cellblocks, dorms, and work sites for the men in our class to sign and asked Ms. Treanor to mail it to me.

Several of the men who signed the card had written, "Get well soon Mrs. Morrow." Others wrote more personalized notes:

"You're greatly missed and I pray that you get well soon so you can be about your Father's works."

"First of all, we all miss you. However, please take your time and let that leg heal completely. Your health is paramount to all of us."

"Get well soon. I don't know about no one else, but I miss you."

"There's got to be a good story behind this. Can't wait to hear it! Get well real soon."

"I can't wait for you to come back."

"May God bless you."

"I hope and trust that you get well soon. May God bless you. Heb. 6:10."

"To my teacher with love. Please get well soon."

"I hope when you get this card you are doing ok. But all in all, get well and we all miss you."

"Wishing you the best, please get well as soon as you can, real soon, real soon, okay."

"Praying that you will get well soon and hurry back to school. We miss you."

"God is always with you."

"Get your rest and get well soon. We all miss you and we all are praying for you."

The card and the messages touched my heart and my tear ducts.

\* \* \*

## February

On February 17, I hobbled from the metal detector toward the school in my brand-new black walking cast. Just inside the fence, I paused to look across the quadrangle at the now-familiar red-brick building and realized how good it felt to get back to the school and the men.

In the hallway that led to the steps to Center Hall, a row of men sat on a long, narrow, wooden bench pushed against the wall across from the hearing room. I smiled and said, "How you doin'?" to each man as I walked by. The officers who stood at the ends of the bench glared at me, but I saw no reason to be rude just because the men wore handcuffs, apparently waiting to be called for disciplinary hearings. If anything, I thought that warranted a warmer-than-usual smile.

A few of the men nodded or mumbled in response, their faces expressionless, and then I spotted too-tall Mr. Brandon…one animated face in a row of masks. I stopped and said, "Are you OK?" It was a stupid question under the circumstances, but I wanted to let him know I cared and couldn't think of any other words to use.

He smiled and nodded. "Yeah, I'm OK. I'll be back to school soon."

I said, "Well, you take care," and walked on by, speaking to the empty faces on the other side of him as I went. He didn't come to the next class, and the men told me he was on lockup.

At the school, Ms. Gelzer said the new principal, Mr. Wyman, had come on board and wanted to see me in his office. The door from his office to the hallway was locked. A piece of typing paper hung on it with an arrow pointing to the door to the large outer office where Ms. Sullivan, the school secretary, and the two inmate clerks worked. That door was locked, too. Mr. McClellan, one of the clerks, let me in, and I noticed that the copy machine had been moved from the principal's office to Ms. Sullivan's space. The door between the outer office and the principal's office was shut. I assumed Mr. Wyman had someone with him, but Ms. Sullivan said, "No, he keeps the door closed. Wait there, and I'll see if it's all right for you to go in."

Mr. Wyman was short, plump, and matter-of-fact. Thin, gray hair stood in wisps on top of his head. He asked me to give him the test-score history of each of the students in the SUI class and told me he'd cancelled my math lab at the Annex, and then our meeting ended.

The men had better news for me. After three surgeries, the doctors had reattached Mr. Harris's retinas. They'd also removed the lens in his left eye to correct a cataract, but his retinas were too fragile for them to replace that lens or to do surgery to correct the cataract in his right eye. Except for blurred images and light, the man still couldn't see, but at least there'd been progress.

Also, we had a new student, Mr. Baylor. He was forty-nine years old, of above-average height, thin, and wiry. His cheeks and mouth sank in, and he may not have had any teeth; I never saw any.

Mr. Baylor was one of the men from Ms. Treanor's ABE class, and I assigned Mr. Jones-Bey as his reading tutor. It turned out to be a good match, and Mr. Jones-Bey helped Mr. Baylor with his lessons both in class and back on the tier.

Soon after I got back, Mr. Lowery started asking me for a hug. He'd come into the classroom and blurt out, "When're you gonna give me a hug, Ms. Morrow? I need a hug bad."

I brushed him off and toward the end of the month said, "I tell you what. I'll give you a hug when you get your GED and graduate. I'll come to graduation and give you a hug." I hoped that would make him hush, and after a couple more exchanges, it did. He moved on to agitate over something else.

Everything had returned to normal, except for the tension of waiting for the GED test scores. Everybody felt it; nobody mentioned it.

# NINE
## Spring 2004
March

At last! On March 2, the results from the GED exam came in, and we could breathe normally again. Mr. Adams-Bey, Mr. Nichols, and Mr. Taylor-El had passed everything! Before class, I squealed at the three men to come into the staff room and gave them photocopies of their diplomas and score sheets. Tense and expressionless, they read and reread their scores, ignoring my assurances that they'd passed. Finally, their faces burst into smiles, and—after we babbled at each other—they rushed out to tell the other men.

The three men went to the math group that day for the last time, and all through class, laughter rolled down the hall from the storage room. I refused to let myself imagine school without the three graduates.

During class, Mr. Nichols came to the classroom to talk to me—the first time we'd discussed anything except schoolwork. He was twenty-eight, had been tried as an adult at sixteen years old, and had been in prison ever since. Mr. Nichols nearly always smiled. His eyes had a playful sparkle and the kind of scrunch in the corners that will someday cause crow's-feet. He looked as though he expected something good to happen and believed that it had already started his way.

He sat next to me and said, "Do you have a book of poems I could borrow, maybe some from a long time ago? I'm looking for a book like what they might use in college. I like to read poems and try to understand what they mean. The thing I like best is trying to understand what the poet was doing with the imagery. See if I can figure it out."

He talked about poetry with a contented intensity, like an adult dog gnawing on its favorite bone. I said, "I'm sure I have something at home you can use. Just give me until next Tuesday to look through my books."

When I got to school on Tuesday, Mr. Nichols stood in the school hall, waiting for me. I pulled out the book and said, "I used this book in college. I made notes all over the pages, so it's pretty messy. If that's going to be a problem for you, I can bring you something that's less marked-up. I chose this one because it covers a lot of poets and tells about each one."

"No, this is great! I'll read the poems, do my interpretation, and then compare your notes with my ideas." He looked as though the good thing he'd been expecting had arrived.

\* \* \*

The following Thursday, Mr. Taylor-El half-danced into the staff room before class. I didn't give him a chance to tell me why he'd come or to say anything beyond, "Hi, Ms. Morrow." I blurted, "I've got to know. Did you send a copy of your diploma to your son?"

He grinned. "You remembered that! Yeah, I did…the very next day."

I commended him for following through, and he looked down and said, "Yeah." After a pause, he looked up. "I came back to the school today to volunteer to tutor for you. I wants to give something back."

I grinned and gushed, "I can't hire any more tutors, but I'd *love* to have you as a volunteer. The men respect you, and they've seen you succeed at what they're trying to do. You'll be fabulous!" He came to every class after that. Mr. Taylor-El helped the men with their GED materials, but he helped the reading students even more. The clown-cum-leader had the perfect attitude to jolly the men through the rough spots and make their work feel lighter.

\* \* \*

The month moved on with no word about Mr. Harris's eyes. I worried about him, stuck in that cell, not able to see, not able to work, and not able to accomplish anything toward his goals. I asked the class if anyone could get a note to him, and Mr. Perkins stood up next to his desk and said, "Yeah, Ms. Morrow, I'll take a note to Henry for you."

At home that night, I typed the note using font size forty-eight. I told him that if he'd come back, we'd find a way for him to do his classwork, that I was afraid he'd lose some of the skills he'd worked so hard to master, and that completely blind people could succeed in school.

I gave the note to Mr. Perkins on Tuesday. The following Thursday, he sauntered to my desk. "I gave Henry your note, and he say he'll think about it and maybe come down when he's feeling better. The doctor told him he's supposed to lie on the bunk with his face looking at the floor, so he really can't do too much walking around right now."

"Well, please tell him I understand he has to mind his doctor, but I want him to come back as soon as the doctor says it's OK." Mr. Perkins said he would.

Mr. Adams-Bey walked in right after Mr. Perkins—the first time he'd come to school since I'd given him his GED scores. He said, "Ms. Morrow, I'd like to be a whatchacallit volunteer tutor, if you think you could use me."

"Mr. Adams-Bey, that would be wonderful! We always can use another tutor."

He started that day.

As I took roll, I looked up and gave a little squeal. Too-tall Mr. Brandon was by my desk—his first day in class since he'd gone on lockup. He looked OK, just a little pale, but his sparkle and energy had drained away, and his face wore the blank mask of the other men I'd seen on the bench. He sat next to me. "Ms. Tomorrow, before this infraction, I hadn't had an infraction for fifteen years. They'd scheduled me to go to minimum security, and I was looking for it to come along just any day, but this lockup'll put my transfer off. It'll be at least another year before they'll even think about it again." He reminded me of a collapsed tent.

"I'm so sorry, Mr. Brandon."

He nodded, picked up a magazine without looking at it, and shuffled back to his seat.

Mr. Carson and Mr. Jones-Bey had recently quit tutoring to do overtime on their SUI jobs, leaving Mr. Brandon without a tutor. Mr. Wells saw I had a dilemma, and he waited to walk down the Flats with me that night. He said, "Ms. Morrow, I'll take Brother Brandon for a while, until you can figure something out for him. I can tutor him and Brother Edwards at the same time, if it won't be for too long."

"Are you sure you'll be OK with him?"

"Yeah, I can do it for you. I got him. Don't worry about me."

I thanked Mr. Wells, and he turned to his favorite topic...getting out of prison. His penultimate favorite was working with at-risk children. Before or after every class, he'd tell me what he'd done toward his release since our last conversation—written to one more lawyer, to one more person who knew somebody in an influential position, to one more city or state official, to one more staffer in the governor's office, to one more state legislator.

I'd read the manuscript of Mr. Wells' second book, *All Things Must Change*, when I did some editing for him. I learned he'd been convicted of felony murder—he'd been involved in a crime in which someone was killed, but he wasn't the person found guilty of doing the killing. The murder had occurred when he and a buddy had tried to rob a jewelry store. Interrupted by the police, Mr. Wells and his buddy had taken the store owner and clerk at gunpoint and escaped in a police car that stood behind the store with the engine running. After a police chase, they'd been forced to stop at a roadblock where law enforcement officers converged on the car, shooting, unaware of the hostages inside. The officers had shot more than 100 bullets into the car and killed the store owner. Convicted of first-degree murder and sentenced to life in prison, Mr. Wells had started serving the prison term, his fifth, in 1978.

We walked down the Flats together, and he said, "You know what a friend of mine said to me? This is a brother that's out on the streets again, got a real nice wife, got a good job, and bought himself a house; he's doing all right. He told me, 'If you're still in here, then you're not doing enough to get out.' I got to come up with some different things to do, because you still see me; I'm still here. I've decided not to let a day go by that I don't do something to get out of here. I've galvanized my family and friends, and they're ready to support me; make phone calls, come up with money, do whatever it takes to finally get me released."

He stopped walking and looked at me. "I *know* what I did was wrong. I *know* I had to pay, but it seems to me like twenty-eight years in here is payment enough. I don't see what good it's doing for me to do any more time when I could be helping at-risk kids on the street. Now you tell *me*! What's going to do society more good—me in here, or me out there working with those kids?"

We started walking again. "I'm not sure what'll be waiting for me when I get out, but I'll keep my irons in the fire, so if the governor's office or anybody else asks me about what I plan to do on the outside, I'll have something definite to tell them, and I'll be able to earn some kind of a living for myself. You know how bad I want to work with at-risk kids. Really, though, I'd take any job I could find. I don't care if it'd mean putting on a little white hat and selling sandwiches on the corner. After all, I'm not used to making a lot of money in here."

He nodded his head. "We figured it out in the dorm the other night, and it'd take us *forty-six years* working as a tutor in *here* to make as much as somebody working a minimum-wage job uptown would get in *one year*. I'll be able to make it OK."

Mr. Wells and I often walked down the Flats and chatted after class like this, although occasionally, the officers made me wait until they'd locked everything up in the school and walk with them or sometimes wait just until the students and tutors had left the Flats. Those officers said I had to wait because it was the rule. I didn't doubt that, so I didn't argue, but most officers ignored the rule.

One night, the school officer stopped me as Mr. Wells and I walked toward the gate and said, "You'll have to wait and leave out of here with me."

Mr. Wells said, "That's OK. I got her."

"No, she'll have to wait for me. You go on."

Mr. Wells hung his head, shuffled toward the gate, and muttered under his breath, "Humph, be safer with me than she is with you"...probably an accurate statement.

\* \* \*

On the first warm spring night, an officer made me wait for the men to clear the Flats, and then I walked out alone. The officers had opened the windows along the corridor, and some of the men stood in front of their cells, catching what fresh air could make its way through the small openings in the casement windows. I spoke to the men and noticed two people I hadn't seen before.

They stood next to each other behind the bars, leaning against the bars with their elbows on the crossbar and their large hands and arms stuck through the upright bars and into the corridor—big, burly men with medium brown hair in close buzz cuts. Their white T-shirts stretched tight across their chests, and their biceps bulged below rolled-up sleeves that capped multitudes of tattoos in blue, green, and red. I smiled at them, said "How you doin'," and got stony glares from both.

From then on, I usually saw them on the Flats when I left—always together—and I thought of them as "the twins." I continued speaking to the men's stony faces but, walking down the Center Hall steps one night, I thought, *I'm tired of those men ignoring me when I speak. I'm not going to waste any more smiles and words on them.* The old adage, "A smile is never wasted," drifted into my mind and spawned the thought, *Wait a minute, you've focused on what those men* aren't *doing for you instead of on what you're willing to give to them. You'd better get your priorities straight.*

Through the rest of the spring, I spoke to the twins and smiled. They gradually went from stony glares to nods and grunts, to nods and smiles, to a responsive, "How you doin'." Finally, they said, "How you doin'?" before I did. I thought, *Giving is the soul-satisfying part. Receiving in return is only the feel-good piece of it.*

\* \* \*

On the last day of March, Mr. Meyer, the advanced-math tutor, came into the staff room wearing a big frown and said, "Do you think I'm controlling? Somebody told me that last night, and I couldn't sleep afterwards. I thought about it all night long."

I struggled to keep a straight face, but I couldn't hold back a grin when I said, "I can see how somebody might think that."

He gave me a faint smile. "I was afraid that would be your response. I don't think of myself that way, but now that I've gone back over things I've done and thought them through, I can understand how I might give that impression."

His eyes lost focus, his smile faded, and he said, "Taken as a whole, prison is not a good experience, but every once in a while, I see how I've benefited from it. On the outside, I never slowed down enough to encounter and get to know myself. I was usually high, and every waking hour, I was either working my butt off making money or playing golf. At least in here I've had to stop, and that's given me the time and space to take a good look at myself...I've had many personal realizations in prison."

He stood for a while, looking inside at things only he could see, and then looked back at me and said, "Oh, before I forget, I want to let you know I won't be here on Thursday because someone's coming to the prison to host a Seder for us."

I knew a Seder was the traditional ceremonial dinner Jews celebrated at Passover, but his statement puzzled me. I said, "You're having the Seder so soon? I didn't think Passover started until next Monday."

He shook his head. "It doesn't, but in here you accept whatever you can get...with gratitude."

It was a rare moment of humility—for him and for me.

\* \* \*

# April

At a class in early April, I took roll and said, "Mr. Simmons has been absent twice. Does anybody know if he's sick?"

The men looked blank, and someone said, "Simmons, which one's he?"

I remembered that a lot of the men didn't know each other's last names and said, "You know, Bic."

The men whooped. Someone said, "Ms. Morrow, how'd you know his name?"

"I keep my ears open."

Then it started. Mr. Chadwick said, "Ms. Morrow, what's my name?"

"Double C."

Mr. Brandon asked the same question, and I said, "Long-tall."

Another man pointed to Mr. Wells and said, "What's his name?"

"Turtle."

Another pointed to Mr. Hynson. "What's his name?"

"Ren."

And on it went, with laughter and, "Yeah, Ms. Morrow," from the men every time I said a nickname.

Before the next class, Mr. Chadwick came to the staff-room door with a man I'd never seen and said, "Ms. Morrow, tell him. What's my name?"

"Double C."

Mr. Chadwick said, "See. I told you," and both men whooped with laughter and walked away.

Driving home I wondered why the men's glee made my heart sad. Was it their amazement that I'd shown an interest in anything about them beyond the names and prison ID numbers on the callout sheet? Was it that it took so little to bring delight to them in that grim environment? Was it that they had so few occasions for gleeful surprise? I didn't know the answer, but the questions added to my feelings of helplessness in the face of those abnormal living conditions.

* * *

Shortly after that, Mr. Carson, Mr. Brandon's former tutor, came into the staff room before class. "Ms. Morrow, I've thought about it, and I can handle my SUI job and still be your tutor."

If we'd been on the outside, I would've hugged him. Instead, I thanked him, breathed a huge mental *Whew*, and asked him to pick up his old assignments—to work with the math students in our classroom and with Mr. Brandon.

While Mr. Carson was away, Mr. Brandon had asked me for arithmetic problems to do for homework. The day Mr. Carson came back, the two men sat at a small table to my left and reviewed the graded paper I'd just given back. Mr. Brandon scowled at it. Mr. Carson turned to me and said, "Long-tall can't understand why you gave him an *excellent* on his paper when he got so many wrong." Mr. Carson raised his eyebrows, eyes wide.

Mr. Brandon stomped to my desk, waving the paper, and demanded, "Yeah, why did you do that?"

I said, "How many problems did you do, Mr. Brandon?"

He counted them. "Eleven."

"How many did you miss?"

He counted. "Four."

"Well it seems to me any time you do eleven problems and get only four wrong, you've done an excellent job."

I held my breath while he studied his paper, smiled, nodded his head, and went to his seat, head held high. Mr. Carson's face relaxed, and the rest of the class got back to work. I made a mental note, *"Never give the men anything they haven't earned."*

A few classes later, Mr. Carson and Mr. Brandon gave me another lesson. I saw them working with stapled sheets of paper instead of the workbook and asked what they were doing. Mr. Carson said, "This is the commissary order form. He wants to learn to read it."

I felt like a fool and thought, *Of course, when you're trying to teach someone to read, you make sure he's working with material that interests him—not that dumb story about the boy who pats a cat.*

The order form listed the items the men could buy from the commissary, and once a month, they marked their order form and turned it in. These were all things I'd thought the state supplied: soap, shaving supplies, deodorant, shoes, underwear, clothing (after the first set they received on arrival), new bed linen, paper and pencils, over-the-counter pharmaceuticals, and snacks.

I thought, *Obviously, he'd be motivated to learn to read that,* and made another mental note: *Stay relevant.*

\* \* \*

Mr. Carson started coming to the staff room before class to chat about getting a college degree. I brought him addresses of colleges that offered correspondence courses, and we discussed materials they mailed to him...all saying they wouldn't accept inmates as students.

\* \* \*

About this time, Mr. Wells and Mr. Meyer expressed back-to-back concerns about the young inmates coming into the Cut. Mr. Meyer came to the staff room scowling. "These kids come in here today without a clue. Do you know they're walking around out there with *headphones* on? Don't they know what can happen to them in a prison if they don't watch their backs?"

The following week, Mr. Wells rushed into the staff room with a scowl that matched Mr. Meyer's and blurted, "I don't know about the kids of today, Ms. Morrow. They're out there walking around with their pants pulled down and their underwear showing. When we came in here, we pulled our pants up as high as they would *go*. We just about had our pants up under our *armpits*. We didn't want any sexual predators reading *us* wrong. I don't understand why the kids coming in today aren't as scared as *we* were.

"We did everything we could to signal we weren't interested in same-sex relations, and we'd take on anybody that tried to initiate one. If they want to get in my face about their thing, I'll give them fair warning, but after that, they not dealing with Brother Jihad any more (his Sunni name). They dealing with *Turtle*!

"Some of my people on the street, they tell me those kids out there just as soon shoot you as look at you...then cry because they did it." He shook his head. "I just don't know any more." He picked up my stack of books, said, "Here, let me take these for you," and walked out of the room, still shaking his head.

\* \* \*

Around mid-April, Mr. Taylor-El met me in the staff room and said, "I met with my new case manager yesterday for my annual file review. She was surprised I was still here. I hadn't been written up for an infraction the whole fifteen years I been in prison, and she said I should've been moved out of here a long time ago. She said she'd start the paperwork to get me moved to minimum. I told her go ahead but not to send me out until after June. I wants my mother to see me graduate."

Before I could respond, Officer Cranford, who'd replaced Officer Mason when she moved on, walked out of the staff restroom. As she walked past Mr. Taylor-El on her way to the hall, she said, "Taylor-El, I knocked the toilet paper in the toilet. Go get it out."

I could see he didn't want to do that, and I didn't blame him, but I also could see that he thought he had to; his transfer to minimum security rode on how he handled the situation. He didn't say a word.

I said, loud enough for Officer Cranford to hear, "She knocked it in there, why doesn't she get it out?" but she didn't respond, and I didn't want to confront her directly and get myself fired.

After a silence, Mr. Taylor-El said quietly, "Yeah, she knocked it in there." Then grinning and bobbing, he walked to Officer Cranford's desk. He probably would've tugged his forelock if he'd had one; it was painful to watch. He said, "Why don't you ask the janitor to fish out the toilet paper?"

A few minutes later, the janitor came into the staff room with a plastic bag under his arm and pulling on latex gloves. He didn't look too happy, either, but least he had the right equipment.

The thing that irked me most about the incident was that Officer Cranford was leery of some of the men in our class—Mr. Lowery and others—and she would never have told any of them to get that toilet paper out. But she didn't feel threatened by Mr. Taylor-El and hadn't hesitated to do a power play with him.

Mr. Taylor-El was scheduled for parole twenty-two months from the day that happened. I hoped that going to minimum security would make the transition to life on the outside smoother for him, and after the janitor left, I said as much.

He responded, "I know that's right, and I wants to go to minimum, but right now this graduation's more important."

\* \* \*

The following Thursday, I walked up to the metal detector, and the officer said, "We're on lockdown. We had a stabbing. You can't go in there." We missed school for the rest of the month.

* * *

## May

In mid-May, Mr. Meyer bounced into the staff room wearing an out-of-control grin. "You're going to have to find a new tutor for my math class. Yesterday they told me I can expect to go to the transition unit any day now, but it'll probably be about two weeks."

"That's wonderful news!"

"I'm pretty happy about it! I'll have five years of probation on the outside, but that's all right."

He stopped grinning and shook his head. "I can't think of anybody who's qualified to take over my class, but I'll give it some more thought."

"That's OK, Mr. Meyer. I'm sure Mr. Hynson can do it. Besides, you've got a lot of other things on your mind right now."

"I'm not sure Ren can handle my class. You have to have a lot on the ball to teach at that level."

"You let me worry about that. I'll talk to Mr. Hynson and see if he'd be willing to try. If he is, I'll send him down to observe the group."

Mr. Meyer said, "Okaaaay," and shook his head.

During class, I asked Mr. Hynson if he'd be willing to teach the math group. He was silent for a bit, then said, "I don't know, Ms. Morrow. I was valedictorian of my class, and all, but I ain't sure I remember algebra and geometry and those things good enough to take over the group. Can you give me some time to think about it?"

"I'll give you until next week, but they may ship Mr. Meyer out soon, and we need to have somebody in place when he leaves."

"OK, I'll think about it over the weekend and let you know."

I dreaded what I had to do next. I called Mr. Adams-Bey and Mr. Taylor-El to my desk and said, "I saw Ms. Gelzer today, and she told me Mr. Wyman is going to have just one graduation ceremony a year instead of the usual two. He's cancelled the June graduation and scheduled the one for this year on September 10. I'm really sorry you all will have to wait so long."

Mr. Adams-Bey and Mr. Taylor-El responded together, "That's OK, Ms. Morrow."

"It's not your fault."

"We'll tell Mr. Nichols for you."

"We can wait; we just want to graduate."

Their reassurances only made me feel worse…probably because it showed the maturity scale tipping deeply in their direction.

\* \* \*

Mr. Hynson met me in the hall before the next class. "I got my old math books out over the weekend and tried working some of the problems. I think I can refresh my memory and teach the class. I know you'll be in a bind when Meyer leaves, so I'll try to help you out."

I said, "Super! Go on down to the storage room and observe the class." As he nodded and turned to leave, I said, "And Mr. Hynson?" He looked back. "You'll do fine." He almost smiled.

After class started, Mr. Lowery boomed, "Ms. Morrow, I don't think I'm ever gonna get my GED. You better give me that hug *now*."

"No graduation, no hug. That's the way it is."

After that, the hug requests died out again, and Mr. Lowery went back to staring at me and commenting on the way I looked. I ignored him and thought, *He's just a big showboat.*

\* \* \*

Later that month, Mr. Clark, our oldest student, who usually went right to work, stared into the distance while I took roll. Then he turned and looked at me, his face softened around the edges. "Ms. Morrow, I been thinking. When I get out, I wants to find me a old dog and just set there and pet him. Been a mighty long while since I seen a dog." He shook his head and opened his workbook.

The other men settled down to work, and Mr. Clark came to my desk. "I wonder, could you bring some poems for me to read, some spiritual, gentle-like ones." I said I would, and he said, "I'd be much obliged," and went back to his seat.

Mr. Hynson came in the room about then and sat in the chair next to me...for only the second time since he'd joined us. "Ms. Morrow, I'd like to tell you how I got where I am now, if you want to hear it."

I said, "Sure I would," and tried not to look puzzled.

In a subdued voice, he began, "Well, my parents separated when I was little, and me and my little brother lived with my dad and grandmother in the country in Virginia, but me and my brother spent the summers in Maryland with our mom. That's when I started running with a group of other Filipino kids. When I was in the tenth grade, I moved to Maryland and ran with my buddies almost all the time."

His face held no expression, but his eyes never left my face. "I got into some trouble and decided to go back to Virginia so I could finish school and get straightened out. That was around the first of June. The next week, on my seventeenth birthday, my father told me to stay home from school because he was going to take me to the probation office to sign some papers so I couldn't go to Maryland again.

"I know now he was trying to do the right thing, but back then I rebelled and went right back to Maryland to run with my buddies. My mom, she was fed up with the things I was doing, and I thought my running buddies was the only family I had left. It was later that month I got locked up."

Mr. Hynson leaned toward me and put his elbows on his knees. "When we were robbing the victim's house, he shot me with a twelve-gauge shotgun. I lost consciousness and woke up in the emergency room. A nurse told me they needed to contact my family to get somebody to sign a consent form for surgery, since I was too young to sign, and she asked me how could she get in touch with my mother.

"I said, 'I don't have a mother.'

"She asked how to get in touch with my father.

"I said, 'I don't have a father.'

"Then when I came to after surgery, my whole family was there at my bedside. A friend heard I'd been shot and got in touch with them. My family's stuck by me, and we've been close ever since. You know, not a one of my running buddies came to the hospital to see me. I realized pretty quick how misplaced my loyalties had been."

I murmured and nodded at what I hoped were the right places, mesmerized.

He continued, "The judge said the murder victim had shot and incapacitated me, so I couldn't have fired the bullet that killed him. Then the judge said I was guilty of felony murder and sentenced me to life in prison plus thirty years."

Still expressionless, Mr. Hynson leaned back in his chair. "When I got sent to prison, I ran wild. You wouldn't believe how I did. Finally, an old hand took me aside and told me I had a choice. I could keep throwing my life away, or I could make something of myself. He talked to me real straight. After that, I looked at myself in the mirror and ain't like what I see. I decided right then to go to school, and I ended up being the valedictorian."

He nodded and smiled. "When I stood up there giving the valedictorian speech, I saw a look in my parents' eyes that I ain't see there before. That's when I realized that when I do good, it affects my whole family, and when I do bad, it affects my whole family. I started working harder to turn my life around, and I had only one or two infractions after that. They were for disobeying a direct order, but I ain't had an infraction since November of 1995."

I said, "How many infractions did you have before that?"

With a big, indulgent smile, he said, "A lot."

He stood up. "Well, I just wanted to share that with you. I'd better get on back to the math class before Meyer starts wondering where I am." Then he walked out.

Driving home that night, I tried to find an explanation for Mr. Hynson's true confession. Maybe he trusted me with his story because I trusted him to teach the math group. Maybe he'd just wanted to talk.

# TEN
## Summer 2004
June

The first week in June, Mr. Meyer walked into the staff room with an armload of books. "I don't want to take anything from here out with me, so I'm giving all my stuff away. I thought the guys might enjoy these books, especially the Westerns. I'd planned to bring some of my historical romance novels, but when the guys on the block heard I was giving them away, they were gone in no time. They're almost as popular around here as soap operas."

I laughed. "You're kidding me, right?"

He stopped smiling, "No, I'm serious. We love those things in here."

I decided not to pursue that tidbit—not even on the ride home that night—but I knew I'd never shake the first image that came to my mind...the twins on their metal bunks, reading Victoria Alexander during a commercial break on "All My Children."

* * *

In mid-June, Mr. Meyer walked into the staff room with slumped shoulders...no smile on his face, no sparkle in his voice. "This waiting is starting to get to me. I haven't been to sleep for three nights. There are so many thoughts in my head, and I can't pin any of them down as thoughts at all. You know, I think it's harder to go out than it was to come in—because of the uncertainty.

Coming in, sure, you know it's going to be bad, but at least you know you'll have a bed and food and heat in the winter."

I assumed that when people got out of prison they could choose among an abundance of halfway houses and said, "Have you tried to find a post-release program to take you in?"

"You wouldn't believe how many letters I've written. I've gotten in touch with every place I could find, and they've all been full."

"Have you tried contacting people in the Jewish community centers? I know they run service programs."

"They said I'd have to contact them after I'm released, but that doesn't do anything to help me find a place to go when I walk out of the gates. It looks like I'm going to be homeless and have to sleep on the streets." He didn't whine. He stated a fact.

Walking down the hall to class, he continued, "My father's wealthy, but he says he won't help me…that I'm on my own. Can you believe that?"

I nodded, "Actually, yes. Sometimes parents have simply given all they can."

He hesitated, then said, "You're right."

\* \* \*

The next week, Mr. Meyer told me, "One of the guys on my wing got out after he'd been in a while. He got a construction job, and the boss told him to go across the street to the fast food place and get coffee for everybody. It was a four-lane road, and he said there were more cars than he'd ever seen, going faster than he'd ever seen. He had to go back and tell his boss he was too scared to cross the street. That ripped him up."

That echoed a conversation I'd had with Mr. Wells a short time before, when Mr. Wells had charged into the staff room and barely given me a chance to say, hello before saying, "Ms. Morrow, I called my aunt last night, and her little son answered the phone. I said, 'Where's your mother?' He said, 'She's out in the yard.' I said, 'Go get her and tell her to come to the phone.' Then he told me, 'I don't have to go get her, I'll take the phone out there.'

"Ms. Morrow, what's up with that? Can you just unplug the phone and take it outside now?"

I explained cordless phones to him, and that led to a chat about the challenges that long-term prisoners face when they get out. He told me about a friend of his who'd been released after he'd served twenty-nine years of a life sentence before DNA proved he hadn't committed the crime.

Mr. Wells said, "He told me about going to the store to buy a tube of toothpaste for the first time after he got out. He thought he'd have two or three kinds to pick from, like when he went in, but there was shelves and shelves of toothpaste. He said he looked at those shelves and almost busted out crying. He didn't know how to choose. He had to leave out of there without his toothpaste."

Driving home, I fumed over the callousness of the prison system and the society that ignores it. Why do we dump people who've been in prison back on the streets with no preparation for success? How can we keep people in a totally abnormal environment for so many years and then expect them to function in a normal one—an environment that's so radically different from the one they left all those years ago? Why aren't there more programs to address this? I pulled into my driveway, immersed in a now-familiar feeling of helplessness.

* * *

Toward the end of the month, Mr. Meyer said, "You know, I'm beginning to believe they're not even going to send me to prerelease. This morning, my case worker put me in a transition class here at the Cut. I'm not sure what to think, and I can't get anything definite out of her."

Mr. Meyer's class lasted a very short time…a day or two, as far as I could tell. I knew they didn't tell him the things he needed to know, because after the program ended, he asked me, "Do you know whether my driver's license is still good?"

"How long ago did you come in?"

"Eleven years ago."

"I doubt that it is, but I'll find out."

He couldn't make a call to the division of motor vehicles to get the information himself, because the men could make only collect calls, which the DMV wouldn't accept. I got the information for him and told him, "The woman I talked to at the DMV said you'd have to retake the written and the driving tests. She'll send me the book you need to study. She also said you'll need your birth certificate."

He didn't know how to get a birth certificate, and I made a call to ask for that information, as well. I wondered what people did who had no one to make calls for them.

I didn't stop to think that I might break prison rules when I made those calls, any more than I did when Mr. Meyer said, "Ms. Morrow, would you mind writing a letter of reference for me...a to-whom-it-may-concern that I could use when I apply for a job?"

"Of course not. I'd be happy to." I'd been a supervisor for twenty years, and that was a natural thing for me to do for an employee who planned to look for other work. Ms. Gelzer told me later she'd gotten in a lot of trouble for writing a letter of recommendation for one of her tutors.

Toward the end of class that day, Mr. Hynson sat next to me and told me about an IMPACT session they'd had the day before. IMPACT, Inmates Making a Positive Attempt to Collectively Educate Teens, was a program run, under the direction of Sergeant Ruth Johnson, by inmates who'd completed a ten-week training session. According to their brochure, "the members (talk) about drugs, peer pressure, responsibility, choices, prison life, education, decision making, self empowerment, etc."

I said, "Mr. Hynson, I didn't realize you participated in IMPACT."

He said, "Yeah, when Sergeant Johnson asked me did I want to be a facilitator, at first I didn't want to do it. I ain't know nothing about kids, and I already had a lot of things going on, but then she told me to think about how I could change their lives and how different my life could've been if somebody had reached out a hand to me. I joined up a few months later.

"When I saw the effect I was having on those kids, it taught me I could make a difference with my life. It's one of the things

that's affected me the most since I got locked up. Another thing
is it gives me a chance to share my poetry. I begin and end each
of the sessions with one of my poems."

"I didn't know you wrote poetry. I'd like to see some of your
poems, if you wouldn't mind showing them to me."

"No, you can see my poems, but I know them by heart. You
want to hear one?"

"Oh, I'd love it!"

He recited the poem to a rap beat:

> If no one does for me…
> I'll pray for myself.
> On my knees prayin'…
> For my freedom, my health.
> Prayin' for strength…
> While playin' the cards I was dealt.
> Now my eyes are bloodshot…
> From all these bloody tears.
>
> Restrained by these chains…
> No one sees that I've changed.
> No one sees that I hurt.
> Things will never be the same.
> Mom helps to maintain.
> Though all I gave her was pain.
> Mom's love still remains.
> I'm the only one to blame.
>
> You trash eaten apples…
> Cuz you ain't know the core is its soul.
> Only ones in my position relate…
> Cuz our souls too have been thrown.
> My heart sheds tears…
> Cuz in prison I've grown.
> In prison I've matured.
> In prison I'm alone.

If no one does for me…
I'll pray for myself.
On my knees prayin'…
To be released from this hell.

\* \* \*

On June 29, I signed a contract to teach for another year at the Cut…an act that felt as inevitable as putting a gold star on Mr. Perkins's paper after he'd corrected his math problems.

\* \* \*

# July

Early in the month, Mr. Perkins waited for me in the hall after class. "Walk out with me today, Ms. Morrow; I've got a surprise for you."

I said, "OK." At the door to the Flats, Mr. Perkins stopped, leaned his head back, and yelled, "*Henreeey!*" The man had a powerful set of lungs, and his voice carried easily to the third tier and Mr. Harris's cell. Mr. Harris shuffled slowly to the bars at the catwalk in front of his cell, and Mr. Perkins yelled, "I got somebody here to see you. It's Ms. Morrow."

Mr. Harris's smile shone from three floors above us. Mr. Perkins turned to me. "Yell something up there so he can know it's you."

I yelled, "When are you going to get yourself back to class?"

Mr. Harris yelled back, "Yeah, that's you, all right. I can't see you, but I *sure* know it's *you*. Right now, I'm supposed to be holding my head still all the time, so I can't hardly come now, but they'll probably call me to go back to the doctor in a week or two, and I'll see about coming to class after that."

"OK. You mind your doctor, but come back as soon as you can. We'll definitely work out a way for you to do schoolwork."

"Well, if anybody can…and *will*…it's you. You won't let *nobody* rest!"

I laughed and said good-bye to Mr. Harris, and Mr. Perkins and I walked toward the gate. I opened my mouth to say how good Mr. Harris looked, and Mr. Perkins said, "Heh-heh-heh,

Mr. Harris say, 'If anybody can and will, it's you. Heh-heh-heh, he say, 'You won't let *nobody* rest.' He's right about that. Heh-heh-heh, I know that's right....''

I dressed my clenched teeth in a smile and struggled to keep the moan in my brain from reaching my vocal cords.

\* \* \*

The next week, Mr. Taylor-El rushed into the staff room, frowning, and blurted, "I don't know what's going to happen, Ms. Morrow. I went to my cell after work, and there was some officers in there boxing my stuff up to ship me out to that minimum-security facility. When I saw that, I nearly died. I couldn't do anything to stop them, but I put in a message to the warden to ask him to postpone the move, and I went to see the security chief. Chief said he'd see what he could do. Ms. Morrow, my mother just *gots* to see me in the cap and gown!"

I mumbled oh-nos and said, "Oh, I hope they'll get the date postponed for you," as I felt my own helplessness merge with Mr. Taylor-El's.

In class, it dawned on me that the security chief wouldn't normally have anything to do with who got shipped out and when, so I asked Mr. Taylor-El why he'd gone to see Chief. Mr. Taylor-El said, "I used to be president of a club in here that Chief sponsored, and we got to know each other through the club. I'm trying everything I know to do, Ms. Morrow. This is too important to just let it slide."

I walked down the Flats by myself that night, lost in a morass of concern for Mr. Taylor-El. When I stopped at the gate and yelled for an unseen officer to come let me out, a prisoner I didn't know walked up behind me and reached across my shoulder. He pushed the gate open and said with a big grin, "You're institutionalized!"

I smiled back at him, but only with my lips. I thought, *Yeah, in more ways than one, and now I've experienced a glimmer of what that means.* The thought squeezed my heart in ways I've never understood.

\* \* \*

Before the next class, Mr. Taylor-El strutted down the hall toward me, grinning. "Chief fixed it, Ms. Morrow. He said I could stay for graduation. Said I might have to wait a while afterwards before I gets to the top of the list again to be shipped out, but that's OK. I been at the Cut a long time; some extra months here won't hurt nothing...not like my mother missing seeing me graduate would."

I hoped Mr. Taylor-El felt the hug of joy embedded in my smiles and squeals.

\* \* \*

I've always felt a particular restlessness when I know there's something I need to do and I'm not doing it. Accumulated feelings of helplessness created that restlessness in me then. It had grown for months. In mid-May, as I drove to the school, the feeling hit full-force, and I tried to think of a way to resolve it. I thought of and then rejected several possibilities: I couldn't start a halfway house...too ambitious; I couldn't create programs within the prison...I taught there; I couldn't open a counseling organization...not qualified. My next thought surprised me: *I know what I can do! I can write a book about the men I've met at the Cut to show that they're everyday people who want to do something positive with their lives, that these are fellow human beings who need our support and encouragement.*

Then the other part of me said, "*Are you nuts?* You can't write a book. You didn't even take creative writing in school!" I rejected the book idea along with the rest and wallowed in my helplessness for the rest of the drive to the prison.

Just inside the classroom, I stopped and said, "Well, look who's here!" Mr. Norman, the man who wanted to be a minister, our first dropout, had come back to school. He reminded me of Georgia cane syrup with its sweet, slow-moving richness—slow smile inching across his face, up his cheeks, and into his eyes; rich, deep voice with a soft Southern drawl; and sweetness in his gentle demeanor.

He turned sideways in his desk to face me, we exchanged pleasantries, and he said, "Ms. Morrow, I been thinking on this a good little while now, and you know what I think you oughta do?"

"No, Mr. Norman, what do you think I oughta do?"

"I think you oughta write a book about us and tell the people out there how we are in here."

My knees got weak, and I wasn't sure I could make it to my desk, but I did, as Mr. Norman said, "Yeah, you know us better than most anybody from outside, and I think you need to tell 'em there're some good people in here. Tell 'em we're not all monsters."

I managed to croak, "OK, Mr. Norman, I'll do that. I'll write that book."

He nodded and smiled and, as he turned around in his desk, said, "I'll see what can I do to help you."

On the way home that night, I drank my iced coffee with the same sense of celebration I felt sipping champagne at a wedding. I toasted Mr. Norman, the resolve to "tell 'em we're not all monsters," and the wonderful feeling that at last I'd been given *something* I could *do* to address the awful, non-rehabilitative conditions in our prisons. I remembered my spiritual director, Sister Patricia McDermott, saying to me, "You have to change hearts before you can change systems." I thought, "Even if my book changes only two hearts, it'll be a start."

# PART II
## NOTES

## Mid-July 2004 to July 14, 2005

The Flats

# ELEVEN
## Summer 2004, continued
Mid-July

I wanted to start working on the book immediately, but I'd signed a contract to teach for another year. I wasn't paid to spend class time working on a book project, but I decided that when I got to my car after a class or when I got home, I'd at least make notes of conversations and events that had happened that night...and regretted, yet again, that I hadn't followed through on my many earlier resolutions to keep a journal.

I also decided to go to courthouses and libraries to research the crimes the men had committed. I hadn't felt a need to know about the men's crimes before, but every time I told somebody about Mr. Harris or Mr. Aloona teaching themselves to read in prison, Mr. Taylor-El's resolve to get a diploma so he could send a copy to his son, or Mr. Wells's successful efforts to write books, the first thing people said in response was, "What did he do?" Except in Mr. Wells's and Mr. Hynson's cases, I had to say, "I don't know." I thought that people who read the book might have questions about the crimes, too, and that I could use those pieces of information to show where the men had been and how far they'd come.[1]

---

[1] After I left the Cut, several of the men told me that they rarely knew the nature of another man's crime—not information they normally shared with each other; therefore, unless I had specific permission from a man to do so, I didn't associate a prisoner's name with his crime in this book.

I started my research close to home, at the Fairview Branch Library. I read accounts of drug deals gone bad, murders, armed robberies, and barroom brawls—probably articles I'd glanced over when the events had happened, but this time, the perpetrators had familiar faces and personalities. The articles gave me a different view of the men, and the words pulled me down into darkness.

I remembered seeing reports of one of the crimes on TV and saying to Ciro that anyone who could act with such disregard for other people's lives had to be beyond rehabilitation. "Get them off of the streets," I'd said, and I also may have mentioned throwing away the key.

My student and his companions had shot from their car to another car. They'd hit their rivals in the other car, but they'd also hit an elderly man in a chair on his front porch, and they'd killed a young mother as she drove her children home from an outing.

I saw my student's name but felt sure that the man I knew was too polite and considerate to have come from the background of drugs and violence that article described...he probably just had the same name as the man who'd done the crime. The article referenced but didn't include a courtroom artist's sketch. The librarian said she'd order a photocopy of it from the library in Baltimore, and I left for the day. I'd had all my heart could take for one afternoon.

The librarian called a few days later to say she had the sketch, and within thirty minutes, I stood at the circulation desk with a knot in my stomach, hoping to see a stranger. I recognized the man and wanted to weep. I'd known my student was as capable of committing murder as anyone else, but the anger and hatred he must have felt contrasted in my mind with the gentle heart I knew.

I wanted to tell him how sorry I was that he'd been in such a raw and ugly place, so far from the person he was capable of being. I wanted to tell him how much I admired him for struggling out of that quagmire and becoming a different person, but I said neither of those things. Instead, I tried to act as though nothing had changed.

\* \* \*

# August

On August 3, a smile played peekaboo on Mr. Meyer's face. He said, "This morning, my case manager told me I'll be getting out of here next week."

"Well, it's taken them long enough, but now you can get to that transition unit and then get on with your life. This is great!"

"No, she didn't say I'd be going to the transition unit. I'm walking out of the gate." For the rest of the day, his mood swung from happy to stunned to fearful and back.

Mr. Meyer came to the staff room before the next class, and his words rushed out like those of a child describing something wonderful. "My dad came through for me. He said he'd pay for an efficiency apartment, give me money to live on, and pay for me to go back to school until I can make it on my own, and he bought some clothes for me to get started with, too.

"He's going to pick me up when I'm released and bring some things for me to change into. They give us a maroon jumpsuit to wear when we leave, but they might as well sew a scarlet letter on our shirts. I told my dad I'm going to change in the car before we leave the parking lot. He wanted me to find someplace in here to change, but they won't let us do that. I'm not leaving the grounds wearing that jumpsuit, though."

His smile broadened. "My dad asked me what I want to do after he picks me up, and I told him I want to go some place to eat where I can order what I want. He said he knows about a deli near here, and I told him that sounded fine to me." Radiating excitement, Mr. Meyer also said that his dad had found a job for him as a tutor with the Volunteers of America.

Tuesday, August 10, Mr. Myer bounded into the staff room and said he'd leave that Thursday, around noon. We grinned and babbled over his good news. After class, we exchanged massive smiles, shook hands, and said good-bye.

My excitement for him carried over to the drive home that night. I thought, *I know what I'll do. I'll get to the prison early on Thursday and wave farewell to Mr. Meyer—like a sports fan waving to a team as it goes off to play the championship game.* By the time I got home, my excitement had faded enough for good sense to kick in.

It reminded me that as soon as the men walked through the gates to freedom, I stopped being a part of their lives and became a part of their past.

\* \* \*

As it happened, I had enough to do that Thursday, anyway. Mr. Wyman had put a memo in my mailbox, a copy of one he'd gotten from Mr. Gillman, the latest full-time teacher in our shared classroom. In it, Mr. Gillman wrote that he wanted us out of his room because the SUI students had taken "two (2) flags, one (1) poster frame, and various school supplies" that belonged to him. Mr. Wyman had written "Ms. Morrow, What Happened!!" across the bottom of the memo.

I thought it seemed awfully strange that people in our class suddenly would start taking things after we'd been in the classroom for more than two years. I said as much to Mr. Wyman, who'd stayed late to talk to me.

Groups of men had been coming to the school at night to take qualifying tests for the four college classes Ms. Gelzer had arranged for the fall, and I told Mr. Wyman I thought it more likely that one of those men had taken Mr. Gillman's stuff. Mr. Wyman responded that he thought it would be best if we moved to another room, anyway. I agreed and left for class.

The officer had locked the door to the room we shared with Mr. Gillman, but some of my students grinned and waved from a doorway farther up the hall, on the other side. They called, "Over here, Ms. Morrow!"

"This is our room now!"

"Look in here!"

Mr. McClellan, an office clerk, had made a sign on the office word processor and printed it on a letter-size sheet of paper, which he'd taped to the wall just outside the doorway where the men stood.

MRS. MORROW'S

SUI/GED CLASS

I hurried over to the men and gushed, "Oh, we have a room of our own!" No one caught the reference, but everybody understood my joy.

We settled into our new space, and I read Mr. Gillman's memo aloud, without comment. The men listened, their faces blank. No one said a word. I continued with class as usual.

A scarred wooden desk in the front of our new room faced the front of the rows of mustard-colored student desks...no more looking at the sides of the men's heads. The desk drawers didn't have locks, so I couldn't leave things in them, but still, it was *my* desk. The stained, orange desk chair had nonfunctioning casters, like the ones in the other room, but it was *my* chair. A green chalkboard covered the wall behind my desk, and an oscillating fan hung beyond reach between two of the windows on the wall facing the door. The windows faced east instead of west, shaded by an adjacent building wing, and we decided it wasn't as hot in there as across the hall. It was a wonderful room!

The men had said the room needed some color, so I brought things to the next class for our walls: a poster that showed the circulatory system in bright reds and blues; a poster with a large red circle, yellow triangle, and bright blue square on a black background; a similarly colored poster that showed basic math functions; a big world map; a big map of the United States; and posters from the American Library Association with quotations from Jackie Robinson ("Life is not a spectator sport...If you're going to spend your whole life in the grandstand just watching what goes on, in my opinion, you're wasting your life.") and Helen Keller ("Literature is my utopia.").

Long-tall Mr. Brandon taped the posters to the walls with double-sided poster tape...so high I could barely reach the bottom edges. We insisted that he put the maps closer to eye-level, and we gave simultaneous directions for the rest.

"Naw, Long-tall, that needs to go over more to the *right*."

"You got that up too *high*, man, we can't even see what it says."

"Mr. Brandon, I believe the circulatory system might do better on the back wall. Let's try it over there."

"That look crookedy to *me*."

Mr. Brandon beamed, adjusted the posters, and moved them around until all of us more or less agreed they looked perfect. We'd marked our territory, and it felt great.

\* \* \*

I continued researching the crimes my students and tutors had committed, and as the horror of their acts clashed with my experience and knowledge of the men, I second-guessed myself. I thought, *Maybe the men I believe I know are characters in my imagination; maybe the men come into the classroom like actors on a stage, playing to an audience of one.* My heart always knew that couldn't be, but my mind worried at the idea and wouldn't leave it alone.

My mind gained an ally from a man in the community where we live, a man I respect. When he asked, "What are you up to these days?" I told him about my teaching. I assumed he'd be a kindred spirit.

He said, "You know it frightens me a little because I think if I got to know some of those men in there, I could be friends with them." I assured him he could and launched into praise for my students.

He abruptly reversed course. "Well, really, I don't see why we should do anything to help them. Nobody helped me. Let them pull themselves up by their own bootstraps like I had to do."

"After a man's been behind bars for twenty years, he doesn't have any bootstraps left to pull."

"They watch TV; they can learn what they need to know to get along after they're released." He smirked and said, "They have conned you! They have you eating out of their hands." I knew discussion would be pointless after that, so I made polite noises and ended the conversation.

A few days later, I gave a ride to an elderly neighbor, and as he got out of the car, he turned and said, "Are you still working at that prison?"

"Yes."

"Well, you be careful when you go in that place. I worry about you being around those men."

I smiled. "Oh, you don't need to worry. They're OK."

He didn't return my smile. "No, they aren't, or they wouldn't be where they are."

I waved good-bye and drove away thinking, *Could the two men be right? Just because my students are fellow children of God doesn't mean they won't deceive me.*

The question pecked at my mind, and it was there the next day, Wednesday, when I flipped through the *Washington Post* Style Section to catch "Doonesbury" on my way to the other comics and the crossword puzzle. A picture and article grabbed my attention—a piece on the death of country singer Johnny Paycheck (August 18, 2004), probably best known for his song, "Take This Job and Shove It."

Bill Friskics-Warren had written that Johnny Paycheck had had many facets. Some, including songwriter, singer, and dignified generous man, were admirable. Others, such as felon and drug addict, were not. Friskics-Warren had concluded that

Paycheck needed to be seen as a totality of those facets, not as a representative of only one.

I read and reread the article, and my mind accepted what my heart had known all along. The positive things I believed about my students were as true as the negative pieces I'd uncovered...and far more numerous. The men were both good people and people who'd done awful things. They *were* trying to pull themselves up, and I cared about them.

I put the paper down and thought about Mr. Norman's plea to "Tell 'em we're not all monsters." There'd been no hint of resentment in his voice, only pain. He probably believed the public had plenty of information to cause fear and even hatred, but he didn't feel animosity toward the people he knew felt so much toward him. He believed that if they only heard the truth, they'd accept it.

It dawned on me that my definition of *Us* had shifted. Those on the outside who thought of people in prison as *the bad guys*—felons and nothing more—had become *Them*. I hadn't come far at all in learning to accept others as myself. So long as I saw *any* group as *Them*, I still had a lot of work to do. I needed to recognize *all* people as a fellow children of God, not merely as representatives of only one of their facets.

\* \* \*

A short time later, I had proof that my caring about the men was more than an abstract thought. It happened the day the wasps invaded our classroom.

As usual on a summer day, the men turned on the fan in our room while I got supplies out of the file cabinet. Before I finished, I heard Mr. Simmons, a large, normally quiet man who was one of our original students, and some of the other men talking to Officer Cranford in the hall. Their words came fast, and I couldn't unscramble them. Then the group came to the staff room, and Mr. Simmons, with a slight, excited stutter said, "Ms. Morrow, there's a lot of wasps in our room, and I don't know if we oughta go in there. Cranford says just shoo 'em out, but there's too many, and we don't want to get stung."

The chorus of men around him added, "Yeah, Ms. Morrow, they's a *whole* lot of them."

"Man, those things'll sting you in a minute."

"Those things're dangerous!"

I went to Officer Cranford's desk with the men following behind and said, "Can you open another room for us, just this once? I really don't want to ask the men to go in a room with wasps. They could get stung. Besides, somebody might be allergic to wasp stings and not know it."

She said, "I can't open any room but the one you're assigned to," and continued to fill out her daily report.

At an earlier time, we could have gone to the storage room where the math group had met, but Mr. Wyman had had the officers lock that door right after Mr. Meyer had left. Mr. Hynson had found a short hallway where the advanced math students took their desks, but it wasn't big enough for the whole class.

Mr. Simmons said, "I don't know, Ms. Morrow; come see for yourself what you think."

I went to the classroom door and peeked in. The room buzzed with the critters as they flew in and out of a hole in the wall—one made for the fan's electrical works but not quite covered by the round fan base. When the men had turned the fan on that day, the wasps had swarmed out in a golden horde from their nest behind the fan. The ones that hadn't returned from their day of doing wasp things outside now flew in through the windows and joined the rest.

We couldn't shoo them out. I knew that stinging things attacked most often at the end of the summer, and all of my mother-hen sensibilities kicked in. I fumed over the thought that the officer had ignored what the men said and had blithely put them in danger.

Turning to the men huddled behind me in the doorway, I said, "We're not staying in here! We're going to the staff room. Everybody go down there and find a place to sit or stand, or if you're comfortable with it, sneak in our room and grab a desk real quick to bring down."

I led the men down the hall and stormed over to Officer Cranford's desk. "We've just changed out meeting place to the staff room."

Her eyes widened, and she blurted, "But—"

"And we'll *continue* to meet in there until *somebody* does *something* to get *rid* of the *wasps!*"

The men had gone into the staff room, and when I stomped in, one of them said, "Aw, don't worry about it, Ms. Morrow. You know her elevator don't go up." Laughter broke the tension, and we settled in for class—the men wherever they could find a space, and I at the wobbly topped table they'd pushed near the restroom door to make a desk for me, complete with my orange desk chair from our room down the hall.

I thought, "It's OK. They're good people at heart. I care about them, and I know it."

The next morning, before I could down sufficient coffee to start functioning and report the wasp situation to the school, Ms. Gelzer called me. "Ms. Morrow, I wanted to let you know that the exterminator has been here and taken care of the wasps. We'll get somebody to clean up, because there are a *lot* of dead wasps in there. You can go back to your regular classroom Thursday."

I thanked her for taking care of the problem and said, "Ms. Gelzer, would you please get a couple of those wasp bodies for me? I see a biology lesson just waiting to happen."

She said, "Sure, I'll do that."

When she gave the bodies to me on Thursday, I taped them to sheets of white paper and labeled the antennae, head, thorax, abdomen, wings, legs, and stinger...probably the only part anybody paid attention to. Things had righted themselves, in the classroom and in my mind.

* * *

Over the next week or so, other dichotomies popped up. But I accepted those better. The first one came up when Mr. Taylor-El asked me about his plant. "Ms. Morrow, I gots this little plant in my cell I'm trying to grow. I had it in a paper cup in some dirt out the yard, but it didn't do very good, so I put in another kind of dirt from over by the compound to try to help it along. It still isn't doing very good, though. Do you know what could be the matter? I mean, I puts the fan on it to keep it cool. I'm hot in that cell, and I know it is, too. I leaves the fan on it when I goes to work."

The men could have ten-inch plastic fans in their cells—bought from the commissary for $25.29...more than a month's wages for the tutors.

I said, "Tell me what the plant looks like."

He grinned. "I don't know, Ms. Morrow! It's green, and it has shiny leaves. You see them all the time in people's offices."

"It's probably a philodendron. If it is, it comes from the tropics, and it loves heat and humidity. It probably doesn't like your fan very much."

He shook his head and chuckled, "Here I am trying to help the little thing, and I'm killing it."

Mr. Baylor said, "I didn't know you was into plants and stuff."

Mr. Taylor-El replied, "I've got a tender side with me! You don't have to be tough all the time, not even in here." It wasn't the tender side that surprised me.

After the next class, an officer walked me down the Flats and asked how things were going in our class. I said, "Great. The men are working really hard, and it's paying off."

He shook his head. "I envy you. I wish I could see these guys the same way you do. When they get in the school, they can put their tough-guy stuff aside because they don't have anything to prove in there. It isn't that way on the Flats. Out here, they all try to act like they're the toughest thing in the jail."

That night, I waited for the car's air conditioner to overcome the heat inside and remembered the former tutor, Mr. Watkins, telling me earlier, "To survive in here you have to have a tough-guy image, and that's the hardest thing for me to do because it goes against who I am."

In the still-hot car, I drove off, wondering why we put people into situations where they have to act like thugs just to stay alive. It didn't look like *rehabilitation* to me.

# TWELVE
## Fall 2004
### September

The Tuesday before graduation, Mr. Hynson ambled into the staff room and said, "Thursday's commissary day, and we want to get a few things to bring in so we can have a little party and congratulate the people's going to graduate on Friday. I know you can't approve it, but I wanted to say something to you before we did anything."

"Mr. Hynson, I don't know about any party, and if one should happen, it would be too late for me to do a thing about it."

"OK. That's cool. All is well."

On Thursday, Mr. Kingsley stuck his head in the classroom to say hi and then walked toward the laughter farther down the hall. About ten minutes later, he reappeared with a sectioned Styrofoam plate piled with food in one hand and a can of soda in the other. He told the men sitting in their desks, "Go on down the hall and get you something to eat," put the plate and soda on my desk, and said, "We thought you'd like a plate, but you might not want to come down there with us."

"Mr. Kingsley, I can't imagine where you got the idea that I'd want to sit here by myself when there's a party going on down the hall!"

A student walked by our door, wisely taking a plate and a soda to the officer who'd pulled school duty that night, and Mr. Kingsley and I left for the storage room. Ms. Gelzer had arranged to have it unlocked for the occasion. Mr. Kingsley put my refreshments on a table and held a chair for me, and I joined the celebration.

A number of the men had made contributions to the party: sodas, small bags of chips or pretzels, cookies, and Little Debbie cakes they'd bought at the commissary—whatever had looked good to them at the time. Mr. Hynson and Mr. Kingsley served everyone from whatever was open when they fixed a plate. My plate had two Little Debbie cakes, two stacks of cookies—oatmeal and chocolate chip—and a mound of party mix. To make the mix, Mr. Hynson had poured chips and pretzels into a clear plastic garbage bag and shaken it to stir things up. The result was delicious.

The students who passed the GED exam had earned the right to be congratulated. According to the American Council on Education's Web site, slightly more than 58% of people who took the GED nationwide in 2003 passed it.

I'd expected a party atmosphere in the room, but although they smiled a lot, the men sat in the assorted broken student desks and chairs, ate their food, and barely talked to each other...except for the men who served the refreshments and Mr. Taylor-El and Mr. Lowery. As soon as the men finished eating, they went back to our room and got to work. Still, the feeling of the special occasion lingered.

I gave plastic portfolios to Mr. Adams-Bey and Mr. Taylor-El but couldn't give one to Mr. Nichols because he wasn't there. I suspected that he didn't want to give up my poetry book.

\* \* \*

Friday, September 10, I put on a new dress and drove to the Cut. Around ten o'clock that morning, Mr. Adams-Bey, Mr. Nichols, and Mr. Taylor-El would receive their diplomas, and I couldn't have been prouder or happier if they'd been my own children.

Two officials who'd come from the state office of education for the ceremony joined me beyond the metal detector to wait for the steel door to open. I knew the man, but not the woman. The man introduced us. "This is Ms. Morrow, the SUI/GED teacher. She loves her students, and they love her."

I smiled, shook hands, and hoped my face didn't show the surprise I felt. I had no idea that anybody outside of the Cut knew anything about our class, other than that we existed, and I'd never realized out loud that I loved those men. The two officials walked ahead of me when the door slid open, metal scraping metal, and I walked to the chapel in a daze.

An officer waved me into the chapel, where Ms. Gelzer—in charge of the day's events as always—rushed up to me and said, "Adams-Bey isn't going to be here. He said to tell you. I don't understand what happened, but Warren Hynson does. He's waiting for you." And she dashed off to get another man into his cap and gown.

Mr. Hynson stood as close to the chapel door as the officers would allow, and he started talking before I reached him. His rapid-fire street rhythms were even more staccato than usual. "Ms. Morrow, Adams-Bey said tell you he ain't come today, and he wants you to know because he ain't want you to be looking for him and he ain't show up. I tried to talk to him last night to get him to change his mind, but he says he's not coming, and now I don't guess there's anything we can do."

The expression on his face said, "Please, do something!"

My heart sank. What had happened? In class the night before, Mr. Adams-Bey had been more excited than I'd ever seen him. Hardly able to stop smiling, he'd said, "I'm gonna see you at whatchacallit graduation, Ms. Morrow," and later, "I'll be there, Ms. Morrow," and then as he'd left for the day, "See you tomorrow morning, Ms. Morrow."

Because Mr. Hynson had gotten his GED in prison, he knew the value of a graduation ceremony with its earned applause, especially in a place that yielded precious few good memories. I also wanted that applause for Mr. Adams-Bey.

I said, "What changed his mind?"

"Adams-Bey's mother said all along she ain't come to graduation, but his grandmother said she'd be here. After school last night, Adams-Bey called her to be sure she knew how to get to the chapel, and she told him she wasn't gonna come. He hung up and found me, and that's when he said to let you know you shouldn't look for him today. He went to work this morning, so he meant what he said."

"Mr. Hynson, what can we do? Can I call his supervisor and ask him to let Mr. Adams-Bey know we want him here? He needs to be here. He worked hard to get his GED, and he deserves recognition for it."

"I don't know what you can do. You probably can't call his job, but maybe you can talk Officer Cranford into calling over there. Adams-Bey probably won't come, but you can try."

Officer Cranford agreed to call, and later I saw her on the phone in a room off of the entrance hall. I didn't know whether she was talking to the supervisor, because I couldn't hear what she said, and I wasn't allowed in the room where she was talking. I waited at the back of the chapel, but before I could catch her eye and motion her over, the ceremony began.

The school staff and teachers had filled the two front rows of pews on the left side of the chapel, so I sat in a pew at the back of that section, behind the graduates' guests, and looked at the banners Ms. Treanor and her committee had painted…"Class of 2004" and "Building a Better Tomorrow," the class motto.

On the podium in a row of folding chairs behind a lectern sat the dignitaries: members of the Cut's administration; Mr. Wyman; Ms. Gelzer, who was the emcee; the representatives from the Maryland Department of Education; and the guest speaker.

Ms. Gelzer had borrowed shiny, royal-blue caps and gowns from another prison to replace the faded rose ones from the year before. The men wore them over their prison uniforms, still one size fits all, but the gold tassels shone, and the caps and gowns looked crisp and fresh. Except for the men who'd gone back to court, the caps and gowns were the only civilian clothes the graduates had worn since they'd come to prison.

Ms. Gelzer started the tape of "Pomp and Circumstance," and the men marched in alphabetical order and took their places in the center pews. I could see all of them…no Mr. Adams-Bey.

Ms. Gelzer introduced members of the school staff, and enthusiastic applause followed each introduction. When she introduced me, the SUI/GED tutors and graduates whistled and cheered; that was fun. As she introduced the guests on the dais, a man in a cap and gown rushed in. His unfastened robe flew out behind him, and he held the cap on his head in a way that blocked his face from my view. He took a seat on the pew behind the back row of graduates, but it wasn't until he turned and gave me a shy smile and a nod that I could be sure he was Mr. Adams-Bey and relax into the joy of the day.

Twenty-two men graduated that day. The ages of the graduates ranged from twenty-two to forty-nine. Mr. Nichols was twenty-eight, Mr. Adams-Bey thirty-two, and Mr. Taylor-El forty-six.

The ceremony mimicked the one the year before. Ms. Gelzer introduced the dignitaries, who received polite applause and came to the dais to say a few words of congratulations—some more than a few—and the guest speaker praised the graduates for the hard work they'd done to earn their diplomas. The exception was the Security Chief at the Cut, who hadn't come to the first graduation.

After Chief congratulated the class of 2004, he said, "I know how long Taylor-El's been working to get to this day, and I know it hasn't been easy. Congratulations, Taylor-El, you did it!" The room erupted with applause, whistles, and cheers, and I could see the left side of Mr. Taylor-El's big grin.

Mr. Wyman called each graduate to come to the front, receive his diploma, and shake hands with the dignitaries. Returning to their seats, some of the graduates waved their hands or diplomas in the air, and all of them smiled. The parents and loved ones cried: tears of joy, tears of pride, and tears for what might have been. I shed a few, myself.

Mr. Taylor-El received his diploma, shook hands, then turned with a big grin and walked up the aisle past his assigned seat. He stopped at the pew where his parents sat, leaned across the two people on the end, and handed his diploma to his mother.

During the ceremony, the inmate kitchen staff set out refreshments on trestle tables covered with white butcher's paper in a narrow room with gray walls and a concrete floor to the left of the podium. This year they'd baked a sheet cake and had potato chips, sugar cookies, and fruit-flavored punch.

After the ceremony, many of the men got their food and went off by themselves to eat. The few men who had guests did not. Those little groups of two or three moved as one unit, Mr. Taylor-El and his parents included. I'd never seen Mr. Taylor-El stand so tall...or so still.

The six graduates who had guests formed a line to have their pictures taken by the prison photographer, and Mr. Taylor-El called me over to meet his parents. Mr. and Mrs. Taylor thanked me, told me how happy they were, and beamed when I said that Mr. Taylor-El had done the hard work and I'd only added the encouragement.

His father said, "He was lazy, though, wasn't he?" It was more a statement than a question.

Mr. Taylor-El said, "Yeah, I have to admit, I was lazy."

I said, "No, I don't remember you being lazy. You had a few off days, like everybody does, but I don't remember you being lazy. You got discouraged. That's why you needed somebody on the sidelines to cheer you on, not because you were lazy."

Mr. Taylor-El grinned. "Yeah, I guess that's right. I did get discouraged, but you pulled me through."

His father, a tall man, mouthed, "Thank you" over Mr. Taylor-El's head. His mother clutched the diploma to her chest with one hand and dabbed a tissue at her eyes with the other.

On a hunch, I said, "Mr. Taylor-El, did you tell your parents you're a volunteer tutor?"

He dropped his head and said, "Nah." His parents looked puzzled.

I turned to Mr. and Mrs. Taylor. "After he finished his classes and passed the GED exam, this man volunteered to stay on and teach other men who needed help." I looked at Mr. Taylor-El. "You work with two reading students now, don't you?" He nodded. "He never misses a class, and he's wonderful with his students. I can't tell you how much he's helping me and the men he's working with."

Mr. Taylor swallowed hard several times, and Mrs. Taylor dabbed at her eyes again. I said it was nice to meet them, and then I walked over to congratulate Mr. Nichols.

Mr. Nichols didn't have guests at graduation, but he smiled the entire two hours. That was how long the men could stay at the chapel before the officers called time and sent them back to their cells—one hour for graduation and one for photographs and refreshments.

Mr. Nichols said, "You know, I'm really enjoying that poetry book you let me use. I don't always agree with your notes, but it's good having them to compare with my ideas." He also asked if he could keep the book for a little while longer. Of course I said yes. I told Mr. Nichols to stop by for his portfolio, wished him well, and went to the gray room for refreshments.

As I walked back into the chapel with my cake and potato chips, Mr. Adams-Bey and Mr. Hynson called me to join them near the front of the photo line, among the families waiting to have a picture made. They also called to Mr. Jones-Bey, who'd been allowed to come because he'd tutored the graduates, and the four of us posed for a picture...just when I'd thought my family had stopped growing.

* * *

At mid-month, still on a high from the graduation, Misters Adams-Bey, Hynson, and Carson, the tutor, came into the staff room together to tell me they'd been accepted into the new college classes. Each man would attend class one night a week—Mr. Hynson on Thursday night and Mr. Adams-Bey and Mr. Carson on Tuesday.

The classes had been scheduled at the same time as ours for budgetary reasons. An officer came to replace Officer Cranford at the end of her shift on Tuesdays and Thursdays because of our class, but on other days, everyone left and she locked the gates and doors at the end of her shift.

Mr. Jones-Bey came to the staff room with the others, and I included him in my congratulations. He said, "No, Ms. Morrow, I'm not going to college. I came back to volunteer again...to help out while you're short on tutors." I could have hugged him.

With Mr. Jones-Bey filling in, Mr. Brandon was my only concern, and I decided to tutor him myself on Tuesdays when Mr. Carson went to class. That worked great, but I had to find something for Mr. Brandon to do while I went over homework with the other men. One Tuesday, I showed him how to do a word-search puzzle in his workbook, and he loved it. I thought the puzzles might help him recognize similar letter clusters when he read and brought him word-search puzzle books. I assigned several puzzles at a time and treated them like any other homework or classwork, writing "Excellent" or "Good" or whatever fit the number of words he missed and giving him a star.

Once when he gave me puzzles to grade, he said, "The men in my dorm see me doing my work, they say, 'Hey, Long-tall, need some help?' and I say, 'Nah, that's all right. I got it.' Because you know I can *do* my own homework." That tooth with the martini glass gleamed.

* * *

Shortly after graduation, Mr. Norman, who'd started coming to class more often, said, "I asked some of the men where I sleep if they'd write something for your book. I thought they might could help you out, but they just too scared of what might could happen if they do it. I don't blame them."

He held out several pages of notebook paper he'd brought to the desk with him. "I made copies of a few things inmates wrote in newsletters and things that I thought you might could use." He'd made the copies by hand, in pencil.

I scanned the pages he'd given me. "These are great. I really appreciate your bringing them to me, but I'd like to see what the other people have to say, too. Tell them they don't need to put their names on anything they write. See if that makes them feel any safer.

"By the way, I ran across a stack of sermons my minister in New Orleans gave back when I lived there. They're old, but what's in them is just as true today as it was back then. Would you like me to bring those in for you to read?"

His face flowed into a smile, and he said, "Yes, ma'am, I'd like to read those, and the men in my Bible study group would, too."

"I want to read them one more time before I give them to you, but I'll have some for you at the next class." That was on Tuesday, and I didn't think about the sermons again until I got my school things together the next Thursday—running late, as usual. I thought, *You won't have time to go to the basement and pull out those sermons, and you sure won't have time to read any. Mr. Norman isn't going to be in class two days in a row, anyway. Why make yourself later than you already are?*

Almost at the front door, I remembered the lesson the twins had taught me. "It can't be about what Mr. Norman will do; it has to be about what *I'll* do, and I promised to bring him those sermons."

I dropped my book bag, purse, and car keys on the entry hall floor, ran to my file cabinet, and pulled out four sermons, thinking, *I'll just have to hope whatever the minister said in these has already sunk into my soul.*

As it turned out, Mr. Norman didn't come to class that day…but this time, I'd remembered the twins' lesson, and it was OK.

\* \* \*

Mr. Norman finally came back for the last class in September, and mid-class, he started toward my desk with a stack of papers in his hand. Mr. Shaw, a stocky, muscular man who acted more like a calf than the bull he resembled, had joined us a short time before. He said, "Norman, whachoo got? Don't tell me you did all that for homework!"

Mr. Norman laughed, "Naw, these is some things I brought to give Ms. Morrow for her book."

"What book is that?"

I told him briefly what I planned to write and why. He stopped smiling and said, "It's important for you to do that, Ms. Morrow, because so many people out there think all people on the inside are mean and evil and not capable of change. Maybe if all fifteen men in this room got out, seven would come back, but what about the other eight?

"Some guys aren't qualified to do anything out there. When they apply for a couple of jobs and get turned down, they may just decide to go back to what they know how to do…robbing or dealing drugs. Maybe they didn't take advantage of the few programs they could do here in prison. But what about the rest of us? That don't mean *we* can't succeed."

I agreed with him and then turned to Mr. Norman, who'd sat next to me, and took his papers. After I'd thanked him and asked him to take my thanks back to the writers, he stayed at my desk. He said, "You know, Ms. Morrow, anything you want to ask me, you can." I did want to ask one thing.

I spent most of my Wednesdays and Fridays in courthouses and libraries, researching the men's crimes, and I hadn't found anything on Mr. Norman after 1967. I asked about the time lapse, and he confirmed he'd been in prison the whole thirty-seven years. He told me things had improved over time, that they used to get a meal only on every third day, with bread and water on the days between, and the prison used to be racially segregated. He said the only thing that had been better then was medical care, because a medical school ran a clinic in the prison, along with a laboratory where they did medical research using inmates.

I thought about Mr. Norman's history lesson as I drove home and realized that the changes he described had come  about because laws had been enacted or enforced. Would it take more laws to force us to do the morally right things regarding our prisons and the people in them?

After dinner that night, I read the papers Mr. Norman had given me—most handwritten but a couple typed on a typewriter with a worn ribbon and uneven letters. None had names or signatures...not even the two in Mr. Norman's handwriting. He'd told me they came from men of all ages.

The men expressed their thoughts in their own words, but each man underscored Mr. Norman's plea to "tell them we're not all monsters" and Mr. Shaw's assertion that people are capable of change. The (mostly) unknown men's words touched and inspired me. Below are excerpts from their papers.

––––––

Each day you struggle against great odds here. Each morning you are reminded of the pressure you're about to face. Faced with all that goes on, I ask myself will I survive another day in here. I learn to pray more and more each day. I know if it wasn't for God strengthening me daily, I wouldn't have survived all these years.

———

Being incarcerated, all you have is time to think. You think about being at home with family and friends and what it was like before coming here. You realize you are getting older now. You become more focused and understand what you never did before. Each day is a precious gift. I ask myself what is my purpose in life? Why was I created? You find yourself asking questions. You're learning now it's time to change the way you think and the way you look at things.

———

Can God give comfort to us in this situation? He can and He does. The God of all comfort comforts us so that we can comfort those in any trouble with the comfort we ourselves have received from God.

———

I'd leave one prison and enter another one. Still there was someone in command, telling you when and what to eat, when you can go outside, when you can shower. They took all your freedom. When I got my time and came to prison I was out of control, seeing how the officers disrespect a man. But now I am at peace within myself since I gave my life to Christ. I am closer to my family outside of this prison, and I am raised up with a brotherly family in Christ here in this prison.

———

Most all improvements in one's life is a choice. Some choose not to grow up and learn from their mistakes while others, like myself, not only learn from our own mistakes but have learned from observing the mistakes and actions of the inmates around us. I view those actions as a reminder to myself of why I'm here now and why I shouldn't take those same actions.

———

I have changed so much since my incarceration. I have matured so much spiritually. I realize how important things are in life such as family, friends, people. I have gained so much knowledge and wisdom of life, God, and who I am as a person. Although it's many negative things around me, because I involve myself in the church, my time is not wasted on negative things.

———

Dealing with my problems usually ended in disaster, but the Lord put my circumstances in a different perspective and has given me peace through the years of incarceration. Yes, and this time will not be wasted, not now and not in eternity.

\* \* \*

## October

After a busy September, we settled into a calmer October...for a while. Early in the month, on a Tuesday, Mr. Hynson showed me another stack of photos from his mom—adults, children, and babies, all dressed up celebrating a family birthday. He smiled as he went through the stack and identified the people for me. Then he said, "That's what keeps me going, right here. That's my heart."

He flipped back through the photos, pulled one out, looked at it for a few seconds, turned it toward me, and said, "My little sister here tells me all the time how strong I am. She says she ain't see how I can be in here and stay so strong. She says she looks up to me; I give her strength. I ain't know how to tell her that all things are not what they seem, that you can be strong on the outside and still be hurting on the inside, so I drew a picture for my sister. It was the head and shoulders of a big bull elephant barely coming out of the darkness around him, and I put a shining tear coming down his cheek. My sister, she looked at the picture and cried. I didn't need to say words."

I said, "Good art is powerful that way. I'd like to see some of your work some time." The next Thursday, Mr. Hynson brought a manila folder of his pencil sketches to class—sparse and powerful pieces.

\* \* \*

Mr. Harris came back to class mid-month, as cheerful as ever, even though he could barely see well enough to get to class and *couldn't* see well enough to read. Mr. Taylor-El and Mr. Jones-Bey took turns working with him and read the exercises aloud so he could give the answers orally. When Mr. Jones-Bey and Mr. Taylor-El needed to work with their regular students, Mr. Harris sat and patiently looked into blurred space.

* * *

Friday, October 15, seven students who'd been in my math lab at the Annex graduated, and Ms. Gelzer fixed it so I could attend. The ceremony was in the library, with Ms. Gelzer in charge but with fewer graduates, fewer guests, fewer dignitaries, and more officers than at the Cut. Officers escorted the graduates in a group to rows of folding chairs. They had no music but did have a commencement address and a speech by the valedictorian, a man whose score placed him high among an elite group of GED graduates nationally.

The valedictorian, who was serving a sentence of life without parole, told the graduates that they'd worked hard to get their diplomas and should continue to work to improve their lives and themselves as much as possible. He gave examples of things they could do, such as helping each other as they'd done when they studied the GED material. The men applauded, and I marveled once again at the caring some of the men showed among themselves.

After the ceremony, officers wheeled in and served cake, ice cream, punch, and potato chips. While we ate, I milled around and spoke to the men from my math lab—all men in their twenties. Four of my students had guests—two whose mother and girlfriend came, a man whose father came, and Mr. Walters, whose mother and sister came.

Mr. Walters, a wiry, vivacious twenty-two-year-old, and his family sat together eating cake and ice cream. As I walked over to congratulate Mr. Walters, he leapt from his chair, knocking it over, and grabbed me in a big hug. He was followed by his mother, whose eyes shone with tears; an occasional one slid down her face. I said, truthfully, "Your son doesn't realize it, but he's a *very* bright young man." A big smile joined her shiny eyes, and she nodded repeatedly, murmuring thank-yous.

Back in the car, my heart broke for the parents who still participated in their sons' lives…children who'd never come home again: the father who'd come to support a son who, in a drunken rage, had killed his two lifelong best friends; and Mr. Walters's mother, who'd watched drugs and the street destroy the dreams she held for her child. I knew the simultaneous smile and tears on Mrs. Walters's face did more to describe the feelings in those parents' hearts than words ever could.

\* \* \*

## November

On a Tuesday in early November, Mr. Taylor-El sat at my desk and said, "You know, Ms. Morrow, before I got locked up, my father paid for me to go to school to be a trucker."

I must have looked surprised, because he chuckled and added, "Yeah, that's right. Then I started doing what I had no business and blew that chance. I wants to try truckers' school again and do it right this time. My father says he'll pay for it." He shook his head, said, "I *gots* to do it right this time," and looked at the floor.

I said, "Well, wanting to's a big part of doing it."

After a pause, he looked up. "That's right, and you know, Ms. Morrow, some of these people in here don't *want* to do nothing when they get out except what they was doing before. They know how to make money doing whatever they did, and that's what they plans to go back to, but a lot of the people in here ain't like that. Like take the brothers in our class, they really *wants* to make something of themselves. They don't want to come back up in here!

"One of the problems is they don't have no programs to help us come up with different ways of thinking—learning different ways of approaching things. See, when people out on the street runs into a roadblock, you all figures out another way to do what you're trying to do or else you figures out a way around that roadblock. You don't keep doing what you did that got you there in the first place. We don't do like you do. We're so used to living with negativity, we just give up or we goes back to an old way of life...something that worked for us before."

He shook his head. "There needs to be some programs in prison for brothers to learn new ways of doing things, and there needs to be somebody or some organization that's there for us when we start running into problems on the outside. We needs somebody who'll help us learn to figure out a productive way to deal with our problems. You know, falling ain't *nothing*. We *knows* how to *fall*. It's staying up that's hard to do."

I knew he was nervous about being back on the street, but neither of us gave it that name. I could only listen and care and try to understand. His fears and the things he'd go through after his release fell way beyond my experience. I had nothing to base any advice on. I understood why so many of the successful reentry programs were run by former prisoners...and desperately wished for more of them.

\* \* \*

The next Thursday, the Cut was on lockdown—another stabbing—and we missed three classes. I took advantage of the time off and left home on Tuesday to research the men's crimes in counties I had to drive two or more hours to reach. I spent the nights in motels and the days visiting libraries and courthouses, leaving them at closing time to pore over the information I'd copied that day.

By Wednesday night, I felt supersaturated with horror stories and pain. I wanted to go home and work in my gardens, to let the blossoms and butterfly wings erase the filth that had seeped into my pores from the case files and newspaper accounts, to immerse myself in the Earth's rich beauty and forget.

By the time the librarian said I'd have to shut down the microfiche reader on Thursday night, I'd convinced myself that the book had been a bad idea, the process was too ugly and painful. I decided I needed to drive to the motel, pack my car, and go home. I wasn't up to the task. As I walked to my car, the voice in my heart said, *You'll be miserable if you don't try to change the way people on the outside see people in prison. If you don't write the book, what else can you do?* I remembered the men's responses when I'd told them about the book, and knew I couldn't let them down. Back in the motel room, I organized the material I'd copied that day, but I didn't make myself read it.

Friday morning, I visited the courthouses and libraries in the last two towns on my list and started home. I tried not to think about the issues I'd wrestled with all week, but my gut churned, and my fast-food lunch sat untouched in a bag on the passenger's seat. I tried to think about plants I'd need to divide when I got home, count the number of beds that needed more mulch, and decide whether I could find space for one more heirloom rose, a creamy peach beauty I'd seen in a catalog.

Those thoughts should have brought contentment, but that day my mind interrupted with questions. How will you face those men when you get back to the classroom? Will you be able to treat them the same as you did last week? Can you look at them without showing revulsion?

I'd learned that four of the men in our class had been convicted of serial rape—one who climbed into windows in the night and one whose crimes also involved kidnapping. All rape is brutal, but another of the men took brutality to a new level, dragging one of his victims down the street by her hair as he drove to the secluded site where he committed even more brutal acts. A fifth man had sexually tortured his girlfriend and ultimately beaten her to death with a work boot in front of her mother. Another had raped his two daughters beginning in their early childhood, and one man had tortured a child over time until the little boy had become too weak to resist and then had drowned the child in a tub of water.

I was sure the crimes I'd read about before that trip caused the victims and their families and friends as much pain as these crimes had, but these grated on my soul even more—perhaps because I felt more empathy for the little boy, the female victims, and the young woman's mother than for participants in a drug deal gone bad or a barroom brawl. Jumbles of thoughts and feelings surged like the bile in my throat. Those women could have been my sister or my daughter or my granddaughter or me. That little boy could have been my son or my grandson. How can I accept the people who might have done these things to us? If I loved the men, wouldn't I betray the little boy and the women whose lives they'd destroyed?

The thoughts continued as I crossed the Chesapeake Bay Bridge. *How can you go back to school and smile at those men? How can you sit next to them and help them with their work? How can you possibly treat those men like you did before? They don't deserve it.*

"They don't *deserve* it?" I detested that statement and had had no trouble seeing the irrelevance of it when other people said it. I knew I'd hate to be blessed only with what *I* deserved, yet that thought had come from me. I told myself, "They say wisdom comes with age, but yours hasn't arrived yet. You've forgotten the lesson the twins taught you, *again*—it's not what others do that matters, it's what *you're* called to do."

Bible verses wove themselves between the thoughts and questions and came to the front of my mind: "He makes His sun to shine on the evil and the good and makes His rain to fall on the just and the unjust" (Matthew 5:45, as I remembered it). And close behind, "Judge not," from Matthew 7:1—that one had always presented a challenge for me.

I thought, *I'm nowhere near capable of the love that kind of acceptance demands, but I need to try to be.* I decided I could accept the men in my class as the people they had become and try to withhold judgment on the men they had been fifteen, twenty, thirty, or forty years before. I had a long way to go to reach that goal, but at least I had a road map.

When I'd started home that Friday, I still had four counties to visit to complete my research. I never made it to those.

\* \* \*

The day class started again after the lockdown, Mr. Carson told me, "Long-tall's going to be on lockup for thirty days."

I blurted, "Is it his *temper?*"

"No, nothing like that. This was for something else."

"Thanks for letting me know."

I left it at that and scurried to class, past college students who stood in small, relaxed groups in the hall with their books balanced on their hips—shoulders squared, heads held high. They discussed algebra, history, English literature, or psychology...in roles that had previously existed beyond their dreams.

\* \* \*

After Thanksgiving break, I unlocked my file cabinet, put the padlock and key on top of the cabinet, as usual, and gathered my books and things, leaving the scientific calculators and other materials in the drawers. Mr. Hynson came in, and we started a discussion that a couple of other men joined. Suddenly, I realized I'd let the time get away from me, so I dashed out of the staff room and down the hall to class.

A short while later, Mr. Baylor ambled in. He'd stopped by the staff room to use the microwave to make popcorn and had seen the padlock and key on top of the file cabinet. He realized what I'd done, locked the cabinet, came to the classroom, and handed the key to me without a word. Then he cocked his head to one side and looked at me with a parental, "You know better than that," expression on his face. I thanked him, and he nodded. He'd saved my hide, and I felt justly but kindly scolded.

Near the end of class, Mr. Jones-Bey, without his usual Italian smile, sat at my desk and said, "Ms. Morrow, I been thinking about it, and I can't understand the men who talk about getting out and driving fast cars and having this jewelry or that and wearing expensive clothes. Man, they *better* be thinking about getting some clothes at the *thrift* store. They better want to go the Salvation Army or someplace like that to do their shopping, or they're going to end up right back in here. You got to be realistic!"

He sat forward in the chair. "My main thing now is just getting myself ready to go out there and live a productive life. I believe the only way I'll succeed is to keep developing spiritually. Without that, man, I don't have any chance. But then, isn't that true of everybody? Without a strong connection to God, you don't have *nothing*! If hard times come, you'll sink right to the bottom. I don't care what your religion is, man, it's necessary to your life." He nodded. "What I've learned is that religion literally means to tie or bind back to the original source and should be reflected in every aspect of your life. I acknowledged a religion before prison, but in name only. Man, my words, actions, and deeds didn't reflect *nothing* Godly.

"I know it's going to be hard back out on the street. One thing is you're going to be on your own out there. In here we have a support system, and the people in it try to keep each other on the right road. Some dudes in here think they can do it on their own, and that's no good, man. That's one thing, too, when you get out, you'd better have somebody on the outside you can turn to, your mother, or your significant other, or your wife, or a good friend, or somebody you can count on. There's got to be somebody who can tell you you're not acting right, because sometimes it's hard to see for yourself."

The officer yelled, "Count's cleared," and ended Mr. Jones-Bey's monolog.

Mr. Wells walked me down the Flats and told me two of his nephews had come to the IMPACT program during the week. His face and voice tightened with emotion, and he said, "That's one time I was *not* gonna miss! I am the *last* member of *my* family to *ever* be in a place like this! If any of the kids in my family start giving them any trouble, I told my people to bring them here to me or put them on the phone with me, because not *none* of us will ever be back up in here if there's anything in my power I can do to stop it! Naw, I'm the *last* one for anything like *this*!"

In the car, I poured hot coffee into my travel mug and thought about Mr. Wells' and Mr. Jones-Bey's words and the emotion behind them. I thought, "Contrary to popular lore, I haven't met a single person who'd rather be in prison than be out."

I screwed the top on my thermos and tried to estimate how much the state would save if it provided programs to help people succeed after their release instead of having to maintain repeat offenders in prison for the rest of their lives—programs to provide places where they could pay room and board and become contributing, taxpaying members of society. I couldn't begin to estimate the savings...not even the monetary ones.

# THIRTEEN
## Winter 2004–2005
### December

December began with heart tugs. The men said Mr. Baylor was in the hospital and would be out for a month—we'd have no way to find out about him until he got back; Mr. Taylor-El still hadn't gone to minimum security, and he told me, "You know, it's really OK. I just remembers the expression on my mother's face when I handed her that diploma, and that makes it worth the wait"; and Mr. Foster read the King Midas story.

Mr. Foster had come to my desk with his book and asked what *grant* meant. He had a short version of the King Midas story in his reading book, with questions to answer after he'd finished. One of the questions was, "If you met Bacchus and he told you he would grant any wish you asked for, what would your wish be?"

I read the question and thought, "What a dumb thing to ask a man who's been in prison for so many years with so much longer to go. No doubt about what *he'd* wish for!"

The afternoon before the next class, I read Mr. Foster's answer at my desk at home. He'd written, "I wud wish for a decent home for my family." I tried to put my heart back together, finished correcting the papers, and drove to the Cut.

At the steps to the school, I stood by myself and yelled for Officer Cranford to unlock the gate. A stocky young man walking down the Flats heard me, came into the tunnel, and stood next to me. I hadn't seen him before and didn't see him after that. He wore a solid white prison uniform, so I assumed he had a job in the kitchen and was on his way to work.

He said a quick, "How you doing?" Then he grabbed the bars of the gate and called, much louder than I had, "Hey, there's a teacher that's in a dangerous situation down here! Are you crazy, or something? Come open this gate!"

Officer Cranford had gone to the office to make copies of her report, closing the door to the hall, and the noise from the machine further drowned out our voices.

The longer the man yelled, the more obscenities and insults he added. I don't remember exactly what he said, except that he mentioned chicken excrement several times in reference to the officer.

I cringed at the thought of what would happen to my benefactor if Officer Cranford heard the things he said. I yelled, "*Hello, Hello*," again and again and hoped the resulting cacophony would mask his words. I also hoped Officer Cranford would respond to my voice before the man got himself any more worked up.

The man stayed with me until we heard the jangle of Officer Cranford's keys in the hallway. Then he waited at the other end of the tunnel, out of her range of vision, until she unlocked the gate. I stepped inside, turned, and yelled "Thank you!" to the empty space behind me, knowing I'd just experienced altruism in action.

The good feeling didn't last long, though. Once inside, I saw signs that Officer Cranford had posted in the hall saying the men couldn't come into the school until 3:45 p.m. It didn't matter that Mr. Fuller had switched our class start time to 3:30 p.m. Officer Cranford had tried to make and enforce the rule before, but this time, Mr. Wyman made it official, and it stuck.

It meant that after the men were released from their cells, they had to wait at the foot of the steps to the school until Officer Cranford let them in. I got to school at the end of her shift, and she often was either in the office doing paperwork or in the restroom when I arrived, causing me to wait in the middle of the crowd of men in the tunnel—the ones she'd locked the gate to keep away from her.

Officer Mason, the officer assigned to the school when I'd started, had locked only the gate at the top of the stairs and had always let the men in immediately. I'd never heard that she had any problems. In fact, a number of men had routinely stood around her desk before class to joke or chat with her.

Officer Cranford allowed only a select few of the college students—none from our class—to stop by her desk, and it took the SUI students a while to realize that she didn't want to interact with them. Mr. Lowery hadn't backed off, though, and someone told me he was the main person Officer Cranford wanted to keep out.

Also, Ms. Treanor was frightened by some of the college students and by three of the men in our class: Mr. Lowery because he stared at her, Mr. Chadwick because of the way he acted toward her, and Mr. Perkins because he looked through the hallway window at her when she used the copy machine. He did that to me, too, and if she'd just turned and waved to him, he'd have given a heh-heh-heh and wandered off. Mr. Lowery caused the most discomfort—both for Ms. Treanor and Ms. Gelzer—because he stared at women. I assumed that he thought he had a smoldering look and thought it quite sexy, but it was so contrived, I brushed it off as an attempt to play, however inappropriate. The other women reacted differently.

Mr. Lowery would stand in Ms. Gelzer's doorway and stare at her. He made her uncomfortable, and I'm sure he knew it. When she stayed late to teach her college class, she asked Mr. McClellan, one of the clerks, to stay in the room with her or she ignored Mr. Lowery, but neither helped.

When Mr. Lowery would stare at me in the staff room, I'd look up and say, "Oh, hi, Mr. Lowery, how're you doing?"

He'd usually say, "Oh, I'm all right. How about yourself?"

"I'm doing great." I think that destroyed the tension he tried to build, and he'd go on his way, usually smiling a little bit.

After the 3:45 rule went into effect, Ms. Gelzer told me that Mr. Lowery had been involved in a violent incident involving officers at another prison some years before and that the incident fueled Officer Cranford's fear of him. I didn't want to think about that—in denial, maybe—but after I heard about the incident, I wondered whether I'd misread his intentions. My intuition said I shouldn't worry about him, but I didn't want to act like a fool. One day, Mr. McClellan, and I were alone in the staff room, and I said, "Should I be leery of Mr. Lowery?"

"Nah, he's harmless. He won't do anything."

I decided to go with what Mr. McClellan and intuition had told me, and I acknowleged to myself that I'd begun to trust some of the men more than some of the officers.

\* \* \*

In mid-December, Officer Cranford let the men in at 3:45, and Mr. Carson loomed into the staff room. His round face looked like a storm cloud. "Ms. Morrow, I'm sorry, but I can't take this any more. Cranford is going to get all of us messed up, and I won't let her put me in jeopardy just because she can't deal with people."

"I don't understand."

His words rumbled out, "We have to come to the school when the officers release us to come, or they won't let us come at all. If we say we have to wait because of what's going on at the school, they'll write us up for insubordination. Then if we come here and we have to stand in the hall and wait for her to decide to unlock the gate, we'll get written up for being in the hall. This doesn't make sense. I can't cope with her and her problems any more. I'm leaving today before they start count, and don't expect to see me back. I hate to leave you and the class, but I won't risk getting into trouble because of her."

I told him how sorry I was to lose him as a tutor but that I understood and didn't blame him for quitting. As he turned to go, I said we'd miss him—what an understatement.

\* \* \*

For the last class before the winter break, I took holiday school supplies to the men: colorful, nine-by-twelve, clear plastic envelopes with small yellow pads, nice pencils, and decent pens inside. I gave the tutors more personalized supplies—art supplies for Mr. Hynson and a plastic accordion folder to replace the tattered paper one that Mr. Wells held together with duct tape. The men's responses warmed my heart and also filled it with sadness. I knew I'd have to leave in June, at the end of my contract, to write the book. That holiday season would be the last I could take school supplies or anything else to the men.

\* \* \*

# January

After the holidays, I expected to see Mr. Brandon grinning from the back row—long after his thirty days on lockup had passed—but he wasn't there. I asked the men whether anybody had heard from him, and from the back of the room, Mr. Foster said, "Naw, but the way I hear he's been yelling all the time, they might as well go on and build him a permanent cage up there."

The men chuckled, and Mr. Wells walked into class. He lived on the same wing as our oldest student, Mr. Clark—the Old Men's Dorm for men fifty and over—and he said, "Ms. Morrow, Brother Clark taken sick here recently, and they sent him out to one of the prisons in Hagerstown, where they got a hospital. I imagine he'll be out a while...may be gone for good."

I thanked Mr. Wells for telling me, and my heart ached. I couldn't do a thing—couldn't send Mr. Clark more spiritual, gentle-like poems and couldn't even send him a get-well card.

\* \* \*

Mr. Carson showed up at the staff room before the next class. "Ms. Morrow, do you have anything Long-tall could work on in lockup? I hear he's pretty bad off, and I think I can get something to him."

"I have some of those word-search puzzles he likes, but are you sure you can do this without getting in trouble?"

"Don't worry about it. I'll be OK."

I gave the puzzles to him, grateful that I'd brought in a big batch of them and hopeful that neither man would feel any repercussions.

\* \* \*

On January 11, I left our room after class, and Mr. Taylor-El called me to join him on the other side of the hall. He was as antsy as I'd ever seen him. We chatted about nothing in particular until everyone had filed by, and then, trying to control a smile, he almost whispered, "I'm rolling out tomorrow. Nobody else knows about it, so please keep it quiet 'til I'm gone, but I couldn't leave here without telling you and saying thank you."

He anticipated my reaction and shushed me before I started squealing. I gave him a two-handed handshake and wished him all the best. His responding smile and nod said he knew I meant it.

* * *

Mr. Chadwick, who'd frightened Mrs. Treanor, had been absent for fourteen of the past thirty-six classes, and I asked the men about him. They said, "He was at work today, but I don't think he's feeling too good" and "I think he's got some things on his mind, but he'll probably be back." At least he wasn't on lockup.

Even without Mr. Chadwick, Mr. Jones-Bey had more students than he could teach, so I tutored Mr. Harris. Mr. Harris would wait at his desk, watching the vague shapes around him, while I went over work with other students, and then he'd come to my desk to do his work. Sometimes precious little time remained, and once or twice, none at all, but that didn't affect his sense of humor or optimism.

The first night we worked together, I noticed him limping and asked him about it. He frowned and said, "That cataract in my right eye's getting worse, and last night, I was on my way to the shower and didn't see the last two steps on the stairs. I fell, and I don't like doing that."

Thank goodness he hadn't hit his head on the concrete, just his knees. I realized it would be frightening, under any circumstances, for someone with recently lost sight and no training to try to get around on his own. In there, where men waited to take advantage of weakness, it had to be even more frightening.

* * *

Toward the end of the month, long-tall Mr. Brandon came back…thinner, with sunken cheeks and eyes. His big smile had dimmed to about a third of its usual wattage, and it stopped at his mouth.

He'd changed in other ways, too. He'd always been a chatterbox, telling tales, making jokes, and asking questions, but after that lockup, he rarely spoke, and then in lifeless tones. Also, except for a couple of slips, he'd been in control of his cursing, but now he blurted angry curse words several times each class. The other men took care of that, but it showed a definite change in his behavior.

In class that night, Mr. Brandon thumbed through one of the sports magazines on my desk. He saw an ad for Jack Daniel's, sat next to me, pointed to the ad, and said, "That was my drink back when I was going downtown and getting in trouble. Yeah, that's where it all started. Every time I got in trouble, it was because I was drinking this stuff.

"My mother used to tell me, 'Boy, don't you go down there and do what you shouldn't,' but I didn't listen to her. About ten years after I came in here, when she and my son was here for a visit, I told her she'd been right, and that if I'd listened to her I'd be home today. I said I was sorry I didn't listen and how much it hurt me to put her and my son through this. They both of them outright cried when I said that."

On the drive home, I decided Mr. Brandon must have done a lot of thinking in solitary. But what else could he do when he couldn't read? Lockup must have been even more horrible for him than for a person who could read the religious material that was allowed and could try to hold on to sanity that way. It hit me that it wasn't only those on the outside who failed to treat people in prison as individuals.

\* \* \*

# February

Before the first class in February, Mr. Hynson got the math group's materials from the file cabinet and said, "Do you know you're getting a new student?"

"I found a sheet on a Mr. H.C. in my box today. Ms. Treanor told me some time ago he wasn't doing well in her class and they were sending him to us. Is that who you're talking about?"

"Yeah."

"I don't know anything else about him—don't even know when he's coming."

Mr. Hynson, who knew just about everything that went on at the Cut, said, "He's supposed to come to class *today*." Mr. Hynson grinned and chuckled, and that made me a little nervous. He went on, "He's different. I mean, he is who he is. He's OK; he's just a little…well, you'll see for yourself. All in good time, you'll see. It's all good."

Mr. H.C. exploded into the classroom that day with a big smile and belted out, "You must be Ms. Tomorrow! The Lord is blessing me each and every day! Happy birthday to *you*!"

I belted back, "And a happy birthday to you, too!" thinking, *This is going to be fun.*

Forty-five years old and stocky, with a smooth face and shaved head, Mr. H.C. wore a white T-shirt, gray sweatpants, and work boots with no laces. When I asked him if I could use his real name in this book, he said, "You know, I'm a clown at heart. I have love for everybody in my heart, too. I guess that makes me a holy clown. That's the name I want you to use for me, aka Holy Clown." Thus, I've called him Mr. H.C.

His volume control had gotten stuck on loudest, and he took "animated" to a new level. Highly intelligent, he would've passed the GED exam, but many nights, he had trouble learning, despite his best effort. When he'd make a mistake in math, he'd laugh and blurt out, "I can't believe I did that. I must need me some more Thorazine." Other nights he'd say, "Maaaan, they must've give me too much Thorazine." I didn't know whether his medication caused it, but something definitely interfered with his ability to process his lessons…if not the drugs the infirmary doled out to him each day, then the drugs he'd taken on the street.

After I left the Cut, Mr. H.C. told me he'd worked with a group on the outside that made drugs. It had been his job to test the finished batches, and they'd called him Test Tube Baby. He'd started using drugs at 11 and left home at 14. He'd abused an amazing number of substances, some as common as alcohol and crack and some things I didn't know you *could* abuse—paint thinner?

He said, "My mother and all those people always asked me why did I do such a thing. That's easy to answer, Ms. Tomorrow...it *felt* good."

His comment reminded me of a passage in Betty Ford's *Betty: A Glad Awakening.* She wrote, "I liked alcohol, it made me feel warm. And I loved pills, they took away my tension and my pain."

Mr. H.C. also told me, with justifiable pride, that he'd gotten clean and hadn't abused any substances, including alcohol, for the past fifteen years.

Mr. Harris had said early on, "You can get just about any kind of alcohol or drug you want in here. Oh, now, it may not be the brand or the exact kind you were used to on the street, but it's close enough for somebody that needs it. You'd best believe if somebody comes in here and gets straight, they did it the hard way."

When he said that, shame over my own stupidity enveloped me. I cringed remembering the times Ciro and I had seen a stories of arrests on the news, and I'd said, "Well, at least they'll be in a place where they'll have to dry out and get straight. Maybe it'll stick." Such ignorance!

\* \* \*

At the following class, Mr. Harris couldn't stop smiling. He said, "I was feeling really depressed yesterday and Sunday, but today they called me out to come to the infirmary for my pre-op blood work. That means I'll be going for my next surgery soon. They're doing what they need to do. I'll be looking around here again pretty soon now. Yeah, by time I get paroled out of here, I'll be seeing *good.*

"I'm going to ask to be paroled back to my home state, where I was born and raised. Don't know how I'll get there, but when I do, the first place I'm going to go is to a church. I've been in here so long, I don't know where to go to find work or a place to stay, but they'll know what to tell me at the church."

I said, "Mr. Harris, I think that's a good idea, but you'd probably better have a back-up plan, in case they can't help you."

"What do you *mean* can't help me? I'll have the little bit of money I'm saving from my work. All I'll be asking for is some help in finding me a job and finding a place to stay so I can get on my feet. I'd be happy to wash dishes or flip burgers, and I don't need a fancy room. Humph! I read the Bible, and I don't see nowhere in there where Jesus talked about he couldn't do."

Driving home on I-97, I thought about our conversation. My heart ached for Mr. Harris with his determination and trust. I wanted to help him reach his goals—get settled in a room, get a job, make a new life. I wanted to call people in his home state and find resources for him. I knew that counseling the men wasn't an item in my job description, but it wasn't in anyone else's, either. I sipped coffee from my travel mug and decided I'd do something to help Mr. Harris when he made parole. That soothed my conscience for a while.

* * *

The school went on lockdown for a week and a half because of violence at both the Cut and the Annex. Inmates had wounded an officer and killed fellow prisoners—one as he sat handcuffed in a van, waiting to be taken to court to testify, while two officers sat in the front seat of the van and listened to loud music.

When school opened again, Mr. Harris told me the doctors finally had removed the lens in his right eye, but they hadn't replaced it or the one in his left eye. He saw that as progress, and it probably was, but he still couldn't see.

That night, Mr. Harris and I worked on the word *bygone*. He said, "Oh, I know that word. I try to live that way, you know. After I was in here for a while, I thought about what I did wrong and started feeling deep remorse for it. I was depressed for a long time. Then, after a while, I realized I had to move on from there. I had to build a new life, but I couldn't never let myself stop feeling the remorse, because it's that feeling that's going to make sure I don't do wrong again. I had to move away from it because it won't change what I did, but I can't never forget it. I think that's why I can do my time and not get down so much now."

I thought, *If he can come to those conclusions on his own, what* could *he do with some help and support?*

Ms. Gelzer was still at the school when I was ready to leave. We walked out together and talked about the violence that had caused the lockdown. She said, "Those were horrible things, but it's not like they happen all the time. The media make it seem like this is a violent place, and we know it isn't like that."

I agreed with her then, but driving home, I thought about it. *No, it is a violent place, but that's not all it is. The prison is like the men in it...multifaceted. The positive things Ms. Gelzer and I feel are brought there by the men we know.*

# FOURTEEN
## Spring 2005
### March

At our first class in March, Mr. Hynson told me he'd gotten a full-time job in SUI operating a single-needle sewing machine, where he'd earn between $1.10 and $2.35 an hour. My "That's great" probably lacked sincerity, because he quickly said, "Oh, but I'm still going to tutor. I ain't let you down that way. I just wanted to let you know I'd be working on the compound, and I ain't get paid here any more. My mother insists on sending me money, and I want her to keep her money for herself. I think she will now, but I know she ain't stop as long as I was making twenty-three dollars a month tutoring." I thanked him profusely for volunteering to stay.

\* \* \*

Before our next class, I went online at home to find a new grammar exercise. On impulse, I also checked to see whether Mr. Raymond, a former tutor who'd been paroled, had been able to stay out of prison.

Mr. Raymond, an enthusiastic, baby-faced blond, had gotten his release date and written  to every post-release program he could locate. Like Mr. Meyer, he'd found them all full. He'd told me his parents were separated, and both lived out of state. With no trace of his usual big smile and bouncy optimism, he'd added, "I have friends who'd take me in, but I can't get messed up with them and get in trouble again." He'd come to the Cut because of a parole violation, so he'd known the risks.

As Mr. Raymond's release date had gotten nearer, Mr. Wells had helped him find a job tutoring at Goodwill Industries, and Mr. Raymond's father had agreed to pay for a motel room for him to live in until he got a paycheck and could pay for the room himself. He'd almost run into class to tell me he'd be OK—his big, toothy smile back in place.

He'd desperately wanted to stay out of prison, but I worried whether he, as gregarious and fun-loving as he was, would be able to resist the calls or visits from old friends after he'd spent time alone in a motel room. I'd hoped with all my heart he'd succeed, but the information I found online said he hadn't.

Before class started on March 5, I told the men that Mr. Raymond was in prison again, thinking some of them would be interested. The men sat silent with looks of disbelief. Then Mr. Wells said, "You can't mean that chubby little white boy."

"Yes, he's the one."

With a slight whine, Mr. Wells said, "But I worked with him to find a job and all. He was all set up. I thought for sure he'd make it."

The other men shook their heads and looked at their desks or looked at me with "Say it isn't so" expressions. They reacted as though I'd reported a death in the family.

I mentally kicked myself for being so obtuse. I thought, *Mr. Raymond left the prison with a job, a place to live, and the confidence that this time he'd stay out—a standard-bearer for the other men's hopes and dreams. You came into the classroom like a clumsy oaf and stomped on those dreams. You blithely announced that Mr. Raymond had lived out their worst nightmare.*

I probably should have apologized for my insensitivity, but I was too busy beating myself up to think to do it.

* * *

By mid-March, I knew I had to take steps to leave the Cut and contribute whatever I could toward resolving problems in our criminal-justice system—at a minimum, writing a book to say, "They're not all monsters." I told Mr. Wyman I wouldn't renew my contract and why. As a department of education employee, even one under contract, it would've been untenable for me to write about the school. Also, I needed to interview the men, and to do that, they'd have to put me on their visitors lists. That couldn't happen so long as I was a teacher. So I handed Mr. Wyman my letter of resignation. He asked whether he could change my mind; I said he couldn't. He said he wanted a written statement of my intention to write a book to forward to the department of education; I said OK, and the conversation ended.

In the classroom, I walked to the front of my desk, leaned against it, and said, "This is something I really hate to say out loud, but I don't want you to hear it from anybody else. I've just told Mr. Wyman I'm leaving in mid-July. That's four months away, so I'll be here a while longer, but I wanted to give him time to find a replacement for me. You're all doing so well, and I don't want to leave you without a class." I'd rehearsed my speech a dozen times on the way to work but found it hard to deliver. I didn't want the men to feel betrayed, and I didn't want to finalize my decision to leave.

I reminded the class about the day Mr. Norman had asked me to "tell 'em we're not all monsters" and told them I planned to make good on my promise to Mr. Norman. I said, "You know how a lot of people out there feel toward you all, and you know how desperately more programs are needed in here and post-release. I've realized that people on the outside won't give the support that's needed for those programs until they understand the individuality and humanity of people in here. The book is the only thing I can think to do to address that. The thing is, I can't write the book while I'm a teacher in the prison system."

The men responded, "We sure will miss you, Ms. Morrow."

"We need you in here, but we need you more outside."

"People won't listen to us, but maybe they'll listen to you."

"We're just glad you stayed for as long as you did."

"You've got to follow your heart."

I thanked them, went back to my chair, fumbled with my papers, took a few deep breaths, and, once composed, called Mr. Lowery up to go over his work.

Before we could start, he said, "Ms. Morrow, this is going to be my last class with you. I'm about eight years into an eighty-five year sentence, and I need to have this GED before they'll give me a job in SUI. I've decided to go to school full-time in the daytime so I can finish up my schooling and try to get me a better job."

I said I thought he'd made a wise decision and, thinking I might not have another chance to talk to him, asked, "When you did your crime, were you into drugs?'

He looked at me like I'd lost my mind, and I thought, *OK, no way he'll answer that one.*

He chuckled and shook his head. "Of *course* I was! You know, I can't blame anybody for what's happened to me. I did it to myself. When I was high, I was violent."

In his book *High Society: How Substance Abuse Ravages America and What to Do About It,* Joseph Califano writes, "Some eighty percent of adult inmates incarcerated for felonies and of juvenile arrestees are involved in drug- or alcohol-related offenses or have drug and alcohol problems." My experience yielded closer to 100%.

That class was also the next-to-last one for Mr. Aloona, but I never could find out why he quit.

Next, Mr. Foster, who'd moved on from the King Midas story, handed me his homework and then stood by my desk. I asked what he needed. Without a trace of his usual shy smile, he said softly, "I almost didn't come to class tonight, Ms. Morrow. I haven't been to work for two days. I had a death in my family."

"Oh, Mr. Foster, I'm so sorry. I'm glad you decided to come tonight, though. It probably was good for you to have a little time off from work, but sometimes it helps to get back into our routines, too."

He nodded. I said, "Who was it who passed away, Mr. Foster?"

With tears in his eyes, he whispered, "My mother."

"Oh, Mr. Foster, I'm so sorry! Will you be able to go to the funeral?" I'd read in Mr. Wells's book that he'd gone to his mother's funeral. He'd entered after the service started and stood shackled at the back of the church with an officer. I didn't know that in 1995, the prison system had ruled that prisoners couldn't attend funerals. Ms. Gelzer later told me that the rule had come down because of attacks on the officers at funerals by some of the inmates' family and friends.

Mr. Foster's chin trembled, and he replied, "No, and that's the hurtingest part of all. I won't be able to go see her."

I said again how sorry I was, and he nodded and left, needing to get back to his desk.

Near the end of class, Mr. Foster sat at my desk with his book and asked me a question about a story. I answered the question, and he read the story aloud. That was a first. When he finished reading, I asked him to read something else, and I pronounced the problem words for him instead of asking him to sound them out. It was as close as I could come to giving him a hug.

\* \* \*

Mr. Harris missed several classes but came back near the end of the month. The doctors had replaced the lens in his left eye but hadn't given him the lens for his right eye or his reading glasses. Still, if he sat far enough from the board, he could see the big letters I wrote and read the words instead of hearing them. I worried that he'd strain his eyes, so we took breaks, especially when his good eye started to water, and I looked forward to his musings then.

On his first day back, he said, "With some of these men, you know in a few minutes why they're in here. Some of them snap at anything, and some of them are just plain mean. Then there's the rest of the men that you can't figure how in the world they ended up in here. Of course, a lot of them are like me and wouldn't have gotten in here if it hadn't been for alcohol, some of them drugs, but when they're straight, they're just as nice as you please.

"I feel like this, here: You got to get it together and find out who you are. You *got* to know who you are in a place like this. If you don't know who you are, you can get lost. Some people come in here saying they're not getting out anyway, so they can be as mean as they want to be, not realizing they're just asking for trouble. There's always going to be somebody meaner than you. If you know who you are, you can tell yourself you never have been mean, and you don't have to *get* mean to survive. That's not who you are. You don't have to lose your soul to make it in here."

I cringed at the thought of living in an environment where the possibility of losing your soul would be a part of daily life.

The good news that day was that Mr. Harris could see better in one eye; the bad news was that Mr. Brandon was on lockup again. The men told me about it, and I blurted out, "That man can't stay *off* of lockup! What in the *world* is he *doing?*"

One of the men gave me a half-smile and said, "Aw, you know how it is. Sometimes they do a shakedown, and they find something in somebody cell they say didn't ought to be there, and they lock him up for it, or sometimes somebody be owing somebody something, like maybe they had a little wager or something, and then the man can't afford to get whatever it was he wagered—you know, like from commissary. Then, maybe the man want to avoid the other dude or lay low until he be transferred or things cool off, so the man do something crazy to get himself locked up for a little while, or maybe the man shoot off his mouth to an officer before he thought it out."

I assumed that was his way to politely say it was none of my business. I let it drop; however, when Mr. Brandon came back, he said it actually was all of the above.

Mr. Brandon also said that soon after he'd gone to prison, he'd been on lockup for four and a half years. He'd had only a couple of magazines, a pencil, and some paper with him in his cell—this man who couldn't read.

I said, "Oh, Mr. Brandon, that must've been awful. I don't know how you stood it."

He looked into the space over my right shoulder for a few seconds, looked back at me, and murmured, "You adapt."

\* \* \*

Before the next class, I looked up and saw Mr. Lowery, standing by my desk, staring. "Mr. Lowery, what are you doing here? Your classes were over hours ago."

"I came by to get my hug. I'm not gonna be in your class no more, and you're not gonna be here when I graduate, so I thought I could come by and get my hug in advance."

I had to laugh. "OK, Mr. Lowery. I'll give you that hug."

Sitting in my chair, I held my arms up, and he bent at the waist to put his face next to mine. We patted each other on the back, and he said, in the softest voice I ever heard him use, "You take it easy, Ms. Morrow."

I said, "You take care now," and he hurried off to get to his cell before count started. He'd been a royal pest, but I missed him.

* * *

At the end of the month, Mr. Wells walked to the staff room with me and said he'd finished his second book. He'd arranged for the proceeds from the book to go to the family of the jewelry store owner killed during the robbery. Mr. Wells often walked with me to the staff room and watched my things while I went to the restroom. Usually, he stood in the doorway between the staff room and the hall, but that night when I came out of the restroom, he was out in the hallway, looking back and forth.

His face broke into a big smile, making his cheek pouches pop up like marshmallows. He said, "I'm doing double duty tonight. The officer asked me to watch her things while she checks the locks. That makes you feel good. You know, it's not just everybody that gets asked to watch people's things, and it makes you feel good when it happens to you. Makes you feel like somebody trusts you."

While the officer finished locking up, Mr. Wells and I headed down the Flats. He said, "Last night in the Old Men's Dorm, we were talking about how it is we've been able to stay in prison so long—some of us over thirty or forty years—without going crazy."

"I don't know how you all do it. The thing that amazes me most, though, is how you've kept your senses of humor."

"We've talked about that some, too...the guys in the dorm. For some of these men, it's because they never had any responsibility. They don't know what it is. They came in when they were teenagers. They never held down a job; they never paid rent or had to buy food. They just don't know what it is, so they're happy-go-lucky, even in here."

"The other thing is they don't have memories like an older man would. Twenty-some years after you've come in here as a teenager, you don't have a lot of at-home memories to come up and mess with your mind. I've been sitting in a cell, looking at the walls for twenty-eight years, and the memories I have of being a teenager are gone. It's the memories I made as a man that hurt me."

We stopped at the gates to the Flats, waiting to be let out, and he said, "I sit there looking at the wall, and I can remember how my wife used to smell when she'd come out of the shower in the morning, how she'd spend so much time getting everything just right about her person before she'd go to work. I remember how intent she'd be about getting her stockings just so. Those are the things that get to a man. You know she died since I been in here."

I said I did know...and gratefully walked through the gates to Center Hall to go home as Mr. Wells turned left to go to his cell.

\* \* \*

# April

In mid-April, Mr. Chadwick came back to class, but without his usual grin and hellos. He'd been absent for a month and a half. We went over his homework, and I fussed at him a little, saying he'd fallen behind the reading level he'd reached earlier. He said, "I know, but it looks like I can't make myself do much of anything these days. I haven't worked out in all this time I've been out of class, and I don't go to the [exercise] yard anymore. I get up and go to work and come back and lay on my bed and think about what I done to get me in here."

His voice broke. He looked at the floor and whispered, "I didn't mean to do what I did." After a few seconds passed, he looked up and said, "Any time I did anything like that, I was drunk." He wasn't offering an excuse, just stating a fact. "On the outside, if I wasn't working, I'd be hanging out at Allie's Ally; that's my favorite bar."

The title of a country song, "Let's Get Drunk and Be Some-body," came to mind, and I ached for him. I said, "Do you go to the AA meetings in here?"

"I haven't been to a meeting in four months."

"Maybe it would help if you started going again."

His voiced matched the indignant expression on his face. "I don't need that. My brother, he was messed up, but he didn't go to no AA or NA. He lost everything he had because of drinking and drugging, but he just used his willpower and stopped. Now he's out of prison and he's got everything back again: nice house, expensive car, everything. I just have to be strong and use my willpower, and I can stop doing that stuff."

I wanted to grab him by the shoulders and say, "No, please don't try to do this by yourself! You need all the help and support you can get." Instead, I said, "It sure couldn't hurt to get some help with what you have to do."

He nodded and went back to his desk.

After our conversation, Mr. Chadwick stayed away for another month. I worried about him, frustrated because I couldn't do more.

\* \* \*

In April, I had my only experience at the Cut that even approached being threatening. I'd reached an age where I had to tell servers in cafes that I wanted regular coffee or they'd bring me decaf, so I considered myself immune to sexual advances. Sure, a couple of men had crushes on the teacher and let me know it, but a pointed flash of my wedding ring ended their timid overtures.

That changed on April 18. Officer Cranford hadn't unlocked the gates for the tutors and students to come in, and I worked alone in the staff room. A prisoner who had no connection to our class sauntered into the room and started a conversation. I walked over to check my inbox, next to the restroom door, and he walked with me, saying, "Can you hold water?"

I thought the man had asked for some rather personal information about my bladder and said, "*What?*"

"Can you hold water? Can you keep something to yourself?"

"Well, it all depends on what it is."

He stood too close for comfort and moved in closer, trying to back me into the open restroom door. "I want to have sex wi' chew. Just step on in the restroom, and nobody'll ever know."

"Look, I am *married*, and that is *not* going to happen, so you need to *leave*."

He inched closer. "It's gonna be good. You know you're gonna like it. My girlfriend says I'm too much for her, but it's gonna be right wi' chew."

I ducked around the man. "Leave, or I'll scream for Officer Cranford." She'd gone to the office to copy her report and probably wouldn't have heard me, but the threat worked. He stomped out of the staff room, and I stood in the doorway to the hall—the most public place I could find—to try to get my heart rate back to normal.

One of the teachers had told me earlier that this man had battered and raped three women during a convenience-store robbery. I was grateful he'd asked first and had taken "No!" for an answer...though I was obviously not grateful to *him*. Because he'd accepted my rejection and left the room without trying to touch me, I let the incident slide, deciding I'd report him if he approached me again...touched or not.

He stayed away from me after that, and as incidents go, it didn't amount to much. I almost didn't write about it here, but I didn't want to leave the impression that I could trust all of the men at the Cut the way I did the men in our class.

This incident reinforced something I'd grown to believe about the SUI/GED students and tutors—they must be an elite group, not like most of the rest of the prisoners. The thought gelled in my mind on the day of the incident, and when Mr. Lowery came to the school to chat before class, I said, "Mr. Lowery, aren't the men in our class a special group of people? I mean, they're different from most of the rest of the population, aren't they?"

Mr. Lowery said, "Nah, they ain't special. I think it's that you're special, and you treat them like *they* are, so they act that way."

That sounded suspiciously like one of Mr. Lowery's pieces of flattery, so later I asked Mr. Hynson the same thing, certain he'd confirm my notion.

He said, "No, I don't think they're special. I think they're pretty representative of the population. I mean, there's not no wild, wild people with no respect for anybody, and there's not no gang members in our class like there is in the morning classes, but other than that, they're pretty typical. Ms. Morrow, every tier has some real good people who made mistakes, and it has some other people who are messed up in the head, and that's just the way it is."

I knew he didn't mean people with mental illness when he said "messed up in the head," although, according to the U. S. Department of Justice Web site (www.ojp.usdoj.gov/bjs), more than 50% of the prison population has a mental illness. At least three men in our class took medication for mental illness, and I felt sure all three would've been on Mr. Hynson's list of "real good people who made mistakes." No, he meant the people— mentally ill or not—who had no remorse for their crimes or regard for other people.

On the day of the incident in the staff room, I took roll, still a bit shaken. Somebody asked whether I knew who the new teacher would be and whether I'd get to screen the candidates. I answered no to both questions.

With a mischievous grin, Mr. Baylor, the man who'd brought me the file cabinet key, said, "Can't you put that book thing off for a couple of years and stay here a little longer?"

Mr. Jones-Bey said, "No, man, she has a calling, and she has to follow that. She doesn't have any choice about it."

Mr. Baylor grinned and said, "Well, couldn't you go follow your calling for a month or two and then come on back up in here with us?"

Through the resulting laughter, Mr. Jones-Bey said, "No!"

Mr. Baylor said, "Well, I tell you what, Ms. Morrow, if you turn on TV and see we've taken over this classroom and won't come out, you'd better come on over here and see about us so we can negotiate to get you back."

The banter and laughter around that exchange smoothed away the tension the incident in the staff room had left with me. Mr. Baylor had come to my rescue again.

Before we started class, the men told me Mr. H.C. had been transferred to the Annex. They didn't know why.

That was my last class before I went on a two-week vacation in Italy. I'd gotten permission to work until July 14 to make up the time, even though my contract ended June 30.

On the drive home, I replayed what Mr. Lowery and Mr. Hynson had said when I'd asked if the men in our class were special. I'd desperately wanted to hear that they were different from the rest of the prison population. I mentally paraphrased a line from the movie *The Awakening:* "the alternative—a prison population made up mostly of people with good hearts—would be unthinkable."

I merged onto I-97 and brooded over the brokenness of our prison system, anguished by thoughts of the people in prison who were capable of and desired renewal in their lives, while we systematically denied them the resources to achieve it. My feelings of helplessness returned in the face of it all. Feeling more pain than my heart could hold, I pulled into a shopping mall, called Ciro, and told him I'd be a little late—that I'd stopped to pick up carryout for dinner. It was true I didn't feel like cooking that night, but mainly, I needed to have a few minutes to sit with my eyes closed and pray, mired in the enormity of the injustices we impose.

\* \* \*

## May

Mid-May, Mr. H.C. shuffled into the classroom, frowning and agitated. It was one of only two times he didn't wish me "Happy birthday to you" when he came in.

He said he didn't know why they'd sent him to the Annex and then returned him to the Cut. He also told me that when the officers had boxed up the things in his cell at the Cut to move him to the Annex, they'd thrown away his math books and the folder with all of his schoolwork in it. Earlier, Ms. Gelzer had said some of the officers didn't see school as a priority in prison and some thought there shouldn't even be a school. The destruction of Mr. H.C.'s books and schoolwork confirmed that for me.

I gave Mr. H.C. new study materials, and he settled down to work, but he didn't do much that day. I'm sure he not only felt his loss but also felt violated and helpless to do anything about it…a victim by any other name.

Toward the middle of class, Mr. Harris and I took a break for him to wipe his eyes. I worried that he'd overused them, but he said he was all right. As he wiped, he said, "Let me ask you something. That Scott Peterson has all kind of women writing to him, trying to start something…and with him on death row. Can you explain that to me? I think they're *crazy*. They know that man ain't never getting *out*. I don't know *what's* in their mind."

He finished wiping and looked at me. "Now, say I was to put something in one of those personal ad places. That would be different. Sure, I committed a crime, but I know in my heart that I wouldn't never do that again. I wouldn't use alcohol no more to try to deal with a problem. I have other ways of doing now. Used to be I'd drink whatever I could get my hands on until I'd black out. That didn't solve nothing! If I hadn't a been drunk, I never would've done that crime. Now, I know that's no excuse. I did what I did, but I'm just saying that I never would do it again. I know that!"

I thought, *Lord, when he gets out of here*, please *lead him to a church with people who'll help him.*

\* \* \*

At our next class, Mr. Harris told me he was seeing double in his good eye. He'd gone to a doctor a few days after it started and learned that the implanted lens had dropped. The doctor gave him some eye drops to try to correct it. We went back to doing his lessons orally.

Mr. H.C. came in shortly after Mr. Harris—the second day he failed to wish me a happy birthday. More down than agitated, Mr. H.C. slumped back to his desk and sat without opening his books or folder. Later, he shuffled to my desk and said, "They say I can't be a clown at Family Day this year. I'm *always* a clown, Ms. Tomorrow! I don't know why they don't want me to do it. They say they have somebody better, but really, I don't see how that can be so. I play with the little kids, make sure they get something to eat, wipe their little noses. I take *good* care of them."

The Cut held Family Day in the summer and again in the winter, and inmates who'd been infraction-free for a year could attend, as could members of the men's families, if their names had been submitted and approved far enough in advance. The men paid $7.50 for each of their guests. Excitement always bubbled as the day neared. Our classes became a little emptier the week before because some of the men worked on standing committees to help with planning and preparations.

At Family Day, inmate bands performed, and food was served: cotton candy, popcorn, ice cream, chicken, and French fries. They had a play area with activities for the little ones and games for the other children. The inmates played against the children and always let them win. They also had arts-and-crafts activities and face painters for the children.

Mr. Hynson headed a group that planned and staffed the last two activities, served on the decorations committee, and painted the children's faces. He loved Family Day and told me once, "It's so nice that, after a while, the kids forget they're in a prison."

By the next class, Mr. H.C. had rallied enough to do his work, and he'd regained full speed and volume by the class after that, even though Family Day was scheduled for the weekend following.

On the Tuesday after the event, Mr. H.C. bounded into class grinning. "Hey, Ms. Tomorrow! Happy birthday to you!" I asked him how he was doing, and he replied, "I'm sore all over, all those little children jumping on me when I was a clown." He'd gotten to be the clown, after all. It's hard to make a complaint stick when you're grinning all over your face, and he didn't try much. His voice said the children kicked him and pushed him around and wouldn't leave him alone, but his face said it was the best day he'd had in a long time.

\* \* \*

Toward the end of class, Mr. Jones-Bey came to my desk to chat while his students worked. He made small talk, and then his smile faded. He leaned toward me and said softly, "Ms. Morrow, I got myself into this mess. I know that. Before I got sent up, I decided to get myself straight and went down to the Carolinas, where I have family. I got a job down there working in a construction labor pool. I was working twelve hours a day and *loving* it, man. What else I loved besides my job down there was living in the country, away from everybody and being on a farm. I enjoyed that work, too, and loved the peace and quiet and being in nature." He shook his head. "I was happy there, Ms. Morrow. It was a good life.

"Then we finished the construction jobs I was working on, and I had to wait until my boss got more work for me to do. The boss said he'd contact me as soon as the new jobs started up, and you could tell he liked the way I worked. I decided to go back to New York while I was waiting for the new jobs. I got sidetracked by all that money, man, and got back into the same old stuff. That's how I came to be here." He smiled. "When I get out, I'm going to go live in the country. That's where I was happy."

* * *

Mr. H.C. brought photos of Family Day to the last class in May to show me his clown costume. He'd made it from a kitchen uniform, white cotton pants with full legs and a white cotton scrubs shirt painted with peace signs, hearts, and flowers—reminiscent of the Viet-Nam War era. Mr. Hynson had painted little hearts and flowers on Mr. H.C.'s face, all of which took second place to his big, unpainted smile.

Three of the pictures showed Mr. H.C.'s duty station, a play area for the small children with a child-sized plastic basketball hoop next to a concrete-block wall. Mr. H.C. guarded the net and played ball with the little ones and a few older children who couldn't resist the fun. Mr. Hynson saw me looking at the pictures and said, "All the kids love H.C."

After I looked at the photos, the men told me my favorite Family Day story. Mr. Kingsley's daughter was five years old when he went to prison, but he and she had stayed close over the years. She'd become an outstanding high school basketball player—her team had gone to Regionals at the University of Maryland—but Mr. Kingsley had never seen her play. He and some of the other men tried to get permission for him to watch a tape of one of her games, but the administration had said *no*.

That year at Family Day, the men had cleared everyone off of the adults' basketball court and led Mr. Kingsley and his daughter out to play a little one-on-one. The men said almost all Family Day activities had stopped as people had gathered to watch the father-daughter game, and more than one person had shed a tear. Mr. Hynson chuckled and said, "She laid him low!"

# FIFTEEN
## Summer 2005
### June

By mid-June, the oppressive heat had permeated the Flats, and when Mr. McClellan, the office clerk, met me on the Flats and offered to carry my book bag, I gladly handed it over. He put the bag on the table in the staff room, and we chatted while I got my mug from the file cabinet and lifted the lid of the cooler to get ice. It was empty—no ice, no slushy water, no soggy plastic bag.

Mr. McClellan, a calm, soft-spoken man, glared at the empty chest. In a hardened whisper, he said, "She didn't," then strode to the desk where Officer Cranford sat. He didn't raise his voice, and his back was to me, so I couldn't hear his end of the conversation, but from Officer Cranford's protestations, I gathered she'd given our ice to some of her friends. Mr. McClellan turned toward me, and I heard him say, "Well, you could have left *some* for the school. You knew Ms. Morrow had class tonight." He came back to the staff room, picked up my mug, and told Officer Cranford to let him out of the gate.

A few minutes later, Mr. McClellan came back and handed me my mug…filled with ice he'd gotten from a friend in an office farther down the Flats. I marveled, once again, at the ability of some of the men to maintain generosity of spirit in that place.

Ms. Treanor met me in the hall to tell me she'd agreed to teach the class when I left—a huge relief. She'd do an outstanding job, and we all liked her.

A third generous act occurred when Mr. Baylor, the man who'd locked my file cabinet, slipped a can of Slice grape soda and a Little Debbie Zebra Cake on my desk as he walked out at the end of class. I thought that was adorable...his equivalent of an apple for the teacher. It was a hot day, and I put the cold soda and cake in my book bag to have on the drive home.

In the car, I reached into my book bag to get Mr. Baylor's treat, and it hit me that Mr. Baylor's generosity constituted gift-giving. I couldn't accept gifts from an inmate, no matter how well-intentioned. At first I didn't see a problem, I'd just take the goodies back to the next class and return them to Mr. Baylor, with a little, "Thanks, but I can't," speech—good plan, bad idea. I remembered that the officers wouldn't let me bring food in. I sure couldn't explain the situation to them, because that would get Mr. Baylor in trouble. I drove away from the prison and enjoyed my treat.

Mr. Baylor did get the little speech, though, in private, in the staff room. He appeared vaguely amused and, with a nod, said, "OK." He didn't bring any more apples to his teacher.

\* \* \*

June 28, the prison was on lockdown again...another stabbing.

\* \* \*

At the last class of the month, during a break to rest his eyes, Mr. Harris said, "You know, on the street, it's like this here: It's all about pride and ego. Somebody's too lazy to look for work, so he doesn't have a job, and then somebody comes along and tells him he can *be* somebody and have lots of money, and the next thing you know, he's dealing drugs. Then somebody cuts across his territory, and the knuckleheads he hangs out with start telling him, 'If you're a man, you have to take care of that. You can't be any kind of man and let him get away with that. You never know what he's going to do next.' Then you want to prove you're a man, and look what happens!"

He frowned. "They want to stick out their chests, and maybe you're running with some women who like men who stick out

SO AM I

their chests, and the next thing you know, you're doing whatever somebody tells you to do so you can stick out your chest, too. Well, that don't make *no* difference. If they don't know you're a man, there ain't *nothing* you can do to make them believe it for once and for all. You have to keep proving it over and over again, when you really don't believe it yourself."

His voice became tighter, and he leaned forward. "Nah, I feel like this here: What matters is that *you* know who you are, and it don't make no difference what those other people think about you because they can't never know you, anyway. Like these mothers and all that you hear about on the news—I listen to the news every day—the ones who're always saying, 'I can't believe my son's guilty. He wouldn't do a thing like that. I know my boy, and he's not that kind of person.' Well, he may not be that kind of person around you, but you don't know *who* he is when he's with his running buddies."

I said, "I know exactly what you mean. I'll always remember a quote from a book I read in college, something like, 'No matter how much we think we know another, we are still but a face in the window.'"

His mouth didn't utter the words, "Say what!?" but his face did.

I thought, *Would you listen to yourself. This man is talking to you about real life, and you're trying to take him to the world of metaphor. You need to stay where he is and hush and learn.*

He leaned back in his chair. "Humph. Well, I feel like this here: You just have to be who you are, no matter who you're around, and make sure that's somebody you *want* to be. I'm fifty-seven years old and will be older when I get out of here. I just want to find me a job—one in a restaurant would be nice because I could be sure I'd always have food to eat—get an apartment, get some transportation, and find a nice girlfriend. I'm not the marrying kind, but I sure would like to find a nice girlfriend. Then I could save up my money, and every once in a while, I could take a vacation and go to some of the places I really want to see, like the Grand Canyon. I *got* to stay away from those knuckleheads and keep focused on staying free!"

\* \* \*

- 180 -

# July

The month began with another lockdown. This time, one of Ms. Gelzer's tutors had been killed—stabbed in the back as he bent over the sink in his cell to wash his hands.

\* \* \*

When classes started again, the men said it was good to be back in school but even better to be able to take a shower. Perspiration dripped down my face and body, so I understood their priorities.

After I took roll, Mr. H.C. came to my desk, sat next to me, and said, "This algebra is killing me! I work hard at it, too. I don't mind hard work; in fact, I like to work hard, but this is *killing* me.

"I want to work hard when I get out. I've been here so long that this is the only thing I know, but when I get out, I want to be independent. I don't want nary woman supporting me. I know I'm going to be scared, though. When people know your past, they try to use you and push you where you don't want to go."

His look was almost pleading. "I work hard in the tag shop on the compound, and then after dinner, I work in the kitchen, cleaning up the grease and making the chrome and the floors shine. I don't get paid in the kitchen." He smiled. "I do get extra food, though. But it wouldn't matter. I just like to work. Yet and still, it looks like to me, I can't work hard enough to do this *algebra*."

I said, "Mr. H.C., you *are* working hard enough. You're already doing the work you don't believe you can do. You say you can't do these problems, but you've gotten almost all of them right, and when we go over the ones you missed, you work most of them out in your head. You can do this stuff!"

"Yeah, but when I get to the test, I can't do it, so I really must not know how to do it here, either, else why can't I do it on the test?"

I tried to explain about test anxiety and told him Henry Ford had said, "Whether you believe you can or whether you believe you can't, you're right."

We talked about that, and then he looked at the floor, shook his head, and said, "Things was so much simpler in the country. I wish we didn't ever move to the city, where everything always goes so fast. Things was slow in the country, and you could take your time and get things right."

He paused and then looked at me with a gentle smile. His voice softened and slowed. "When I was a little child, I used to get up in the morning early, before sunrise, and work until five-thirty or six in the evening. It was hard work on my grand-mother's farm, but we had it nice. We had horses and cows and pigs, and we raised our own hay and corn for the animals and raised vegetables for us. The horses and pigs was my favorite." He chuckled. "I never did milk the cows too good."

The more he went into the memory, the slower and softer his voice became. He reminisced about his childhood on the farm—hunting with his father, how wonderful the smokehouse smelled inside, and the food they ate: breakfasts of biscuits, fresh honey, and coffee; turnip greens; tall glasses of cold buttermilk with cornbread crumbled in it.

His smile faded. "I want to go back to South Carolina when I get out...get some land I can work and live on. I know the work'll be hard, but I'd like that. My relatives sold my grandmother's farm when she died, but I want to go back and see where it was, even if there's a highway going through it now."

He stared at the corner of my desk, shook his head, and almost whispered, "I don't want fast no more."

* * *

On July 12, my next-to-last day, I went to the cooler for ice, and it was full. Usually, the ice was almost gone when I came in. Then Mr. Kingsley and Mr. Nichols stuck their heads into the staff room to say hi. Mr. Otis, the inmate leader of Ms. Gelzer's writers' group, stopped by to chat, and Ms. Gelzer joined us. I assumed that her writers' group was meeting that afternoon and that my former students had joined.

I left for class and saw Mr. McClellan next to the officer's desk, leaning on a cane. I said, "Mr. McClellan, what in the world happened to you?"

"Oh, it's nothing much. A dude jumped on my foot when I was playing ball, and it's just swollen a little bit." I gave him unsolicited advice about getting off of his foot and keeping it elevated, and he replied, "Yeah, that's what they told me in the infirmary." Before I could fuss at him, Mr. Clark, our oldest student, called to me from across the hall. He'd been in the hospital at another facility for six months.

I hurried over, and Mr. Clark grinned and said, "Hi, Ms. Morrow, I'm back. You know they sent me to the hospital at Hagerstown because they thought I had TB. Then come to find out I had pneumonia, so I stayed there until I got myself straightened out and come back here." He scowled. "When I come back, they'd thrown out all my books and my papers. I'm trying to get back the books that belonged to the school, at least, but the officers said they probably couldn't do me any good. Those books is probably gone. They threw out all my stuff like that, even my school papers that I did in your class. I'm sorry I can't get those books back for you. They did leave me this book that belongs to you personal, though, and I brought it to you." It was a leather-bound Louis L'Amour Western that Mr. Meyer had given us.

I thanked Mr. Clark and asked how he was feeling. He said, "When I got back here to the Cut, they sent me to University Hospital for tests, and when they looked at those, they said I had cancer. That cut right through me when they said it, but you know, after I thought about it, I don't believe it...not a bit of it. I've known too many people who had cancer, and I'm not doing like them."

He stood up straighter. "I'll be seventy-five my next birthday this year, and I think I'm doing just fine. They wanted to shoot that electricity or something though me, but I know all about that, and I won't let them do it. If they do that, it'll make that cancer go all through your body. Yes, it will. So I'll just keep on the way I am."

"Mr. Clark, you really need to talk to your doctor about this some more and ask him to explain things to you."

"Nah, nah, no siree! Don't matter what he says. I'm not doing it. That stuff'll kill you quicker than anything."

Had he been anyone else, I would've tried to change his mind about talking to the doctor, but I knew better than to try with Mr. Clark. Instead, I told him I'd keep him in my prayers.

In the classroom, I saw Mr. Lowery and thought it was dear of him to stop in to say good-bye. Then I noticed a person in the back I'd never seen, but he was talking to Mr. Nichols, so I assumed that he was another member of the writers' group.

The visitors left, and after I took roll, Ms. Gelzer stuck her head in the door and said she needed to take the men to Ms. Treanor's room for a few minutes. Mr. Bickford and Mr. Wyman stood behind her. I thought they were pretty rude to start things with Ms. Treanor before I left, but I said it was OK. Then Ms. Gelzer said, "I'm coming back for you in a minute."

Any dunce would've realized what was happening at that point, but I was stuck on them giving a pep talk to the students before I'd even left, ticked off that they'd cut into our class time. In a minute or two, Ms. Gelzer stuck her head back in to say I needed to come over and join the men, but that hadn't given me enough time to get over my huff and get my brain back in gear.

When we got to Ms. Treanor's room, I saw the men from our class sitting in the student desks, grinning, and the others sitting in desks and chairs off to the side. Almost all of the students and tutors, past and present, were there. Among the exceptions were Mr. Harris, at the hospital about his eyes, and Mr. Brandon, on lockup *again*.

It was a party, and there I stood, dripping perspiration, with no lipstick, wearing sandals, a casual linen skirt, and a T-shirt—clothes I'd picked because of the ninety-plus–degree heat. The part of my hair that wasn't wet stuck out in unruly waves because of the high humidity. That registered with me at about the time I recognized the stranger from the back of our classroom, the prison's photographer…snapping pictures.

Mr. Wells, Mr. Watkins (whom I hadn't seen in more than a year), Mr. Jones-Bey, and Mr. Adams-Bey stood, smiling, behind a trestle table loaded with food, plastic eating utensils, and Styrofoam plates and cups. The cooler filled with ice sat on a chair behind them.

Mr. Wells showed me to my seat, a straight-back chair next to the food table and facing the students, and told me that each of the men wanted to say a few words. I said, "No, they can't do that. I don't have a hankie." Mr. Wells handed me some of the brown paper towels they'd brought for napkins, but Ms. Treanor replaced those with her box of tissues, and the ceremonies began.

Mr. Wyman spoke first, followed by Mr. Bickford, who gave me a plaque of appreciation from SUI. Next, Mr. Otis, from Ms. Gelzer's writers' group, stood beside me and read a poem he and Mr. Hynson had written for the class to give me. It definitely required tissue.

### To Morrow

After giving of yourself and giving of your time
After giving to our lives and giving to our minds
After giving to us knowledge we only planned to borrow
We ask ourselves, "What can we give to Morrow?"
You have given us hope when we have been lost in despair
You have given us strength we never knew was there
You have given us a reason to smile when surrounded by sorrow
And we ask ourselves, "What can we give to Morrow?"
For years you have brought a little piece of heaven into the depths of hell
In the midst of desolate places, you have been a well
You have shared in our travails, triumphs, and our heartbreak
In a place that kills souls daily, you have given us a reason to live
But to Morrow, what could we ever give
Days, months, and years have come and gone
Through personal injury and constant change, you've carried on
As your name Morrow speaks of promises of a new day
We know you will continue to do what you have always done, just in a new way
Traveling the world in search of wonders hidden in distant places
Reading the stories of a million lives etched into foreign faces
So, as our todays become bright and offer the opportunity of the unseen
We can look back upon the nights that pushed us towards the toMorrow of
our dreams
So what can we give to Morrow?
Everything we fail to give today
What can we give to Morrow?
An endless effort in all we think, do, and say
So what can we give to Morrow?
A pledge to forge ahead despite our situation
What can we give to Morrow?
We give our promise to pursue education without hesitation.

While I blew my nose and wiped my eyes, Mr. Jones-Bey put a small table in front of me and Mr. Wells and the other men behind the food table started to serve. They gave the first plate to me and took plates to everyone else at their seats. The men had bought food from the commissary or hustled it from the kitchen. The centerpiece of the table was "hook-up," a jailhouse favorite the men made in their cells with tuna, chopped onion, mayo, pieces of American cheese, and cooked, drained Ramen noodles. They'd brought two disposable aluminum pans of hook-up, garnished on top with a layer of black pepper and a delicately carved tomato rose. They'd called in favors to get a small chocolate sheet cake with vanilla frosting from the kitchen, and they'd made party mix from assorted flavors of potato chips. They also served Ritz crackers, Little Debbie cakes, and cans of Pepsi that they poured over ice in the Styrofoam cups.

While the men served the food, students and tutors stood and made little speeches, beginning with Mr. Kingsley. "I was her first GED graduate, so I want to be the first one to talk. I'll make this short. (Laughter) Ms. Morrow, I had tried other ways and couldn't get my diploma or pass the test, but you got me through it, and I just want to say thank you."

Mr. Adams-Bey, in full voice and with no reluctance, said that he'd tried to get his GED in a number of other classes and hadn't been able to but had come to our class and achieved his goal. He said, "Sometimes we didn't know where Ms. Morrow was coming from, like with all those stars on everything." That got a laugh and agreement. "But then we understood that she knew what she was doing." That got agreement, too...from everyone but me.

Mr. Jones-Bey said, "When I think about Ms. Morrow, it's all about inspiration. She's inspired us to look beyond where we are, to think about other people and places. She's shown us how to be instead of telling us how to be. We knew we could count on her to be here, no matter what, and to be for us."

Mr. Lowery said, "Ms. Morrow, people in here survive by pulling games, but that didn't work with you. We had to be real in your class. And you know some of the times we didn't want to go to class. We'd say, 'It's so hot today, you know Ms. Morrow ain't coming,' and next thing you know, there you'd be on the

Flats, headed for the school. We'd say, 'Awww, man!' and then we'd have to go on to class, knowing all the time that was what we needed to do."

Everyone spoke from beside their desks except Mr. H.C. He stood next to me. He'd painted a big red heart on the back of his T-shirt and painted smaller hearts of different colors and designs on the front. He held out the shirt to make sure I saw the hearts, then quietly thanked me for understanding and patience. I was too sniffly and weepy by that time for the rest of the things he and the other men said to stick in my mind, but I appreciated all of them.

When Mr. Wells finished serving the food, he had his say and then opened a large brown envelope and pulled out a plaque the men had commissioned from the SUI shop—a brass rectangle with lovely black scrollwork in the corners and a black inscription, mounted on beveled cherry wood. Mr. Wells read the inscription, and what was left of my second helping of hook-up got pretty soggy. After the reading, several people told me that Mr. Kingsley had made the plaque. That was special... and then some. Here is the inscription:

---

This Award of Appreciation
Is Presented to:

## Ms. Morrow

For your Unselfish Dedication
towards Instructing and Inspiring
the men at MHC as a Teacher,
Encourager, Friend, Counselor
and yes even as a Mother. For all
that you are to us ... Thank You !!!

---

Mr. Jones-Bey brought the plaque to me and asked me to tell again why I'd decided to leave. He said some of the men hadn't heard the story. I finished blowing my nose and drying my eyes and told them about Mr. Norman's plea to "tell them we're not all monsters," repeating the speech I'd given when I'd told the class I was leaving. I also promised the men I wouldn't use anybody's real name unless I had written permission.

Mr. Lowery said, "You may not know this, but I've never read a whole book in my life. I'll definitely read this one, though." I assured him that I *hadn't* known that or I'd have made certain he read at least one book in our class and reported on it. Guess I hadn't caught every one of his games, after all.

After everyone had spoken, I stood, thanked the men for their remarks, and told them I was the one who needed to say thank you. "Your examples of courage, determination, and strength of spirit will inspire me for the rest of my life."

When I finished and sat down, Mr. Adams-Bey passed a bag of hard peppermint candy, first to me and then to each of the others. He offered the candy bag with all the aplomb of a British butler, as graciously served as any after-dinner mints ever have been.

Mr. Nichols got his mint and came to my table to chat. Just as I told him he could keep the poetry book, the photographer interrupted our conversation and gathered the students, tutors, Ms. Treanor, and me for a group photo. Ms. Treanor and I sat in chairs, and the men stood around us. I held the plaque from SUI, Ms. Treanor held the plaque the men had given me, and Mr. H.C. held an eight-by-ten photo of his mother.

The photographer took fifteen shots of the group—enough to make double prints and give everyone a copy. Then he took multiple photos of me with the tutors and of me with the men who'd earned their GEDs, enough so each person in the picture could have a copy. I couldn't remember many times when I could have held a genuine smile for twenty-five consecutive photos, but that was one. I just wished I'd remembered to put on lipstick and had worn a nicer outfit.

After the photo shoot, the students went back to our classroom, and the tutors stayed behind to clean up. I left Mr. Adams-Bey mopping the floor.

On my way out, Mr. McClellan hobbled over to speak to me, and I told him again to keep his foot propped up. He said, "Oh, it'll be OK. I'm going back to the infirmary to get my cast now, but I waited until I could come to the school to tell you good-bye."

Back in our classroom, Mr. Kingsley laughed, shook his head, and said, "Remember when Ms. Morrow hung all those leaves all over the walls? It looked like a *kindergarten* class in here." We joined his laughter and retold the leaf story for the men who hadn't heard it. That led to sharing memories of Mr. Taylor-El because he'd talked so much about the leaves, and then to remembering the wasp invasion. So it went, as we relaxed after a good meal and relived a shared history, comfortable in a common bond.

On the drive home, I mentally replayed the day and realized that the things the men had appreciated most were that I'd shown up, believed in them, and looked into their eyes. They made me accept, for the first time, that sometimes it really *is* the thought that counts.

\* \* \*

Most of the men came to the last class. We had a normal day, except that we chatted more than usual, and I handed out some farewell school supplies, including magazines and blank journals.

Mr. Harris, back from the hospital, still didn't have the lens for his right eye, still didn't have any glasses, and still saw double out of his left eye, yet he still had faith that he'd soon have good vision again. I thought, *If I ever met an example of hope springing eternal, I met it in that man.*

Count cleared on time, and I stood at the end of my desk as the men walked by in single file. I gave each of them a little hug, and we murmured our good-byes and good wishes. Mr. Baylor cocked his head and said, "One of these days, I'm gonna buy you a soda and a bag of chips and a candy bar."

I smiled. "I'll look forward to that day."

He nodded and walked out.

In the hall, Mr. Clark stopped me. "I want to wish you all the best, especially with that book. If you ever come to a place that you gets discouraged with it, you just stop and realize that I'm praying for you and get your strength from that to go on and do what you need to do. God bless you."

\* \* \*

I think about Mr. Clark and the other men a lot. I write to many, visit a few, and look at their plaques and group photo on my wall. Those things remind me why I needed to write this book—it was the least I could do for my friends.

# EPILOGUE

O n Monday, March 19, 2007, Governor Martin O'Malley announced that, in a surprise move over the weekend, the state closed the Cut permanently and shipped all of the men to other facilities, some out of state. He said the Cut was too dangerous a place to remain in use. Articles in the *Baltimore Sun* show that from August 2002 to August 2006, four inmates were stabbed, five were otherwise attacked and injured, and seven were killed; two officers were stabbed, four were otherwise attacked and injured, and one was killed.

When inmates killed the officer, July 25, 2006, the men went on lockdown and stayed locked down until they shipped out, most for eight months. Many of the men from our class were sent to the Annex, now renamed Jessup Correctional Institution.

I'd often wondered, without wanting to find out, whether I could have loved the men in my class if I or a family member had been the victim of a violent crime. On June 7, 2007, my stepson, who'd lived with my husband and me after our marriage and who'd made the prefix "step" go away, was shot and killed in a road-rage incident. When I moved outside my grief enough to think, I knew that I desperately wanted the killer to be caught and taken off of the streets, but I also wanted the killer to have the programs and help necessary to bring him from where he (or she) was to a place where, if he returned to society, he'd never, ever do to another family what he'd done to ours. None of that impacted my feelings toward the men I knew at the Cut.

As to the men in our SUI/GED class, Mr. Taylor-El and Mr. Meyer are still on the outside, as are Mr. Aloona, Mr. H.C., and the clerk, Mr. McClellan, who finished serving their sentences and were released. Mr. Hannah-Bey developed cancer and died at Jessup Correctional Institution. Everyone else remains incarcerated.

I volunteer with the Maryland Restorative Justice Institute, whose director is Walter Lomax, a man who was released from the Cut after he'd served thirty-nine years of a life sentence for a crime he didn't commit, and, until I was waylaid by an illness, I was a volunteer teacher—the *only* teacher—at the Southern Maryland Pre-release Center.

One day, as I left the pre-release center, an officer at the sign-out desk asked, "Where did you teach before this?"

"I taught at what used to be the Cut and the Annex."

"Whooo-hoo! You couldn't *pay* me enough to work over there. Those are some mean men!"

An inmate who stood at the desk said, "I know *that's* right. Those men are *dirt* mean!"

I smiled and said, "Not *all* of them."

# APPENDIX A

Further all men are to be loved equally. But since you cannot do good to all, you are to pay special regard to those who, by the accidents of time, or place, or circumstance, are brought into closer connection with you.

—St. Augustine

Unless you volunteer or work in a prison, or have family members or friends in prison, you may not have the closer connection with prisoners that St. Augustine described in the quotation above. I wrote this book to provide that closer connection for you.

The people I knew in prison were men; however, I know from my work at the Department of Justice that the conclusions I reached and the suggestions for action I make in Appendix B apply equally to women in prison.

I came away from my experience at the Cut knowing why the major religions and major spiritual movements of the world teach that we are all one and make no exception for people who've committed crimes, however horrible. Most of the men I met were good people who, as a priest named Father Terry Ryan once said to me, "will always be judged for the thing they did on the worst day of their lives." I know I wouldn't want that for myself. I met men at the Cut whom I wouldn't want to encounter on the street, but that didn't make them any less children of God.

We need to improve the conditions in our prisons significantly. More programs are needed to educate and provide job training for people in prison and to help them adjust to society after years of incarceration. I know, however, that not enough programs will be provided, not enough money will be appropriated for them, and not enough citizens will be found to support them, so long as people in prison are considered to be different from people on the outside. Gratefully, individuals and organizations have responded to the need and are trying to help, but so much more is needed.

I don't say that every person in prison can become a productive member of society. Some can't because they don't want to. Several men at the Cut told me about people who are doing their time so they can get out and go back to the things they did before their convictions, usually something involving robbery or drugs. Those people believe they were good at what they did, and they made a lot of money at it. They see no reason to change. It's their chosen career. If they killed someone along the way, they think of that as an occupational hazard. Other men have mentally or emotionally gone to a place that may be beyond our reach.

The men I taught were trying to improve their lives, some because they wanted to be better qualified to get jobs after they were back on the street, some—who had no hope of release—because they wanted to do something positive for people they loved or because they wanted to grow as people. I know that the men in our class never, ever wanted to do anything that would put them back in prison, if they were released, and 95% of people in state prisons are released.[2]

It definitely would be in society's best interest if they didn't repeat their crimes.

One of the remarks I hear repeatedly from people on the outside is, "Why should we educate those people? They don't deserve it. Some of them will never even get out, so we're just wasting our money on them."

---

[2] U.S. Department of Justice, Office of Justice Programs, Bureau of Justice Statistics, www.ojp.usdoj.gov/bjs/prisons.htm

I believe that every person has a sacred right and obligation to become the best person he or she can be and that we all have a sacred obligation to help each other achieve that. Additionally, a recent three-state study showed that people who are educated while they are in prison are significantly less likely to return to prison when they're released,[3] and a second recent study found that education prevents almost twice as many crimes as continued incarceration when the same amount of money is spent on each.[4]

We on the outside don't need to do anything to punish people in prisons. I promise you that the prison system is taking care of that. But you and I need to see the men and women in prison as our brothers and sisters, just as we need to see everyone else in the world. This is not only for the sake of people in prison. If we can't see them as fellow children of God, we can't hope to save our society or our individual souls—not theirs, *ours*.

All of the major world religions and spiritual movements teach that we must love everyone as though we were they:

- Jesus said, "This is my commandment, that you love one another as I have loved you."[5]
-  In the Torah, it's written, "You shall not take vengeance or bear a grudge against your countrymen. Love your fellow as yourself."[6]
- Muhammad wrote, "You will not enter Paradise until you have faith, and you will not complete your faith until you love one another."[7]
- Confucius wrote, "What you do not want done to yourself, do not do to others."[8]

---

[3] Steven J. Steurer, PhD, Linda Smith, PhD, and Alice Tracy, PhD, "Three State Recidivism Study," Correctional Education Association, 2001, www. ceanational.org

[4] Audrey Bazos and Jessica Hausman, "Correctional Education as a Crime Control Program," UCLA School of Public Policy and Social Research, 2004, www.ceanational.org

[5] *The Holy Bible*, New Revised Standard Version, John 15:12.

[6] Leviticus 19:18, www.jtsa.edu.

[7] *Spirituality: Passage in Search of the Heart of God*, edited by Jude Patterson, Barnes & Noble Books, New York, 2003.

[8] Ibid.

- Hafiz wrote, "Everyone is God speaking, why not be polite and listen to him?"[9]
- A passage in the Bhagavad Gita states, "The wise man, cleansed of his sins, who has cut off all separation, who delights in the welfare of all beings, vanishes into God's bliss."[10]
- Gandhi wrote, "All men are brothers and no human being should be a stranger to another. The welfare of all...should be our aim. God is the common bond that unites all human beings. To break this bond even with our greatest enemy is to tear God himself to pieces. There is humanity even in the most wicked."[11]
- The Dalai Lama wrote, "Love for others and respect for their rights and dignity, no matter who or what they are: ultimately these are all we need."[12]

The above quotations address the saving of our souls. What about society?

On June 30, 2008, 2,310,984 people were imprisoned in the United States, a number that increases every year.[13] In 2005, we spent over $68 billion in prison-related costs in this country.[14] That number also is increasing, and that isn't even the most alarming statistic. According to the FBI's *Uniform Crime Reports*, 1,318,398 violent crimes were committed in the United States in 2009. That's at least 1,318,398 people—plus untold numbers of

---

[9] *The Gift: Poems by Hafiz the Great Sufi Master*, translation by Daniel Ladinsky, Penguin Compass, New York, 1999.

[10] *Bhagavad Gita: A New Translation*, translation by Stephen Mitchell, Three Rivers Press, New York, 2000.

[11] *All Men Are Brothers: Life and Thoughts of Mahatma Gandhi as Told in His Own Words*, compiled and edited by Krishna Kripalani, Columbia University Press, New York, 1960.

[12] *Ethics for the New Millennium*, His Holiness the Dalai Lama, Riverhead Books, New York, 1999.

[13] U.S. Department of Justice, Office of Justice Programs, Bureau of Justice Statistics, www.ojp.usdoj.gov/bjs/prisons.htm

[14] Ibid.

family members, friends, and neighbors—who were affected by crime.[15]

The statistics are beyond alarming, and we must pay attention to them. At the same time, we mustn't turn the war against crime into a war against the people who committed the crimes. That hasn't led to a solution for our crime problem and shows no sign of doing so; nor has it served to prepare people who are released from prison for life on the outside. A study in the *New England Journal of Medicine* found that "during the first two weeks after release, the risk of death among former inmates was 12.7 times that among other state residents." The leading causes of death were "drug overdose, cardiovascular disease, homicide, and suicide."[16]

Isn't it time we tried another approach? During the years I taught at the Cut, I realized that the correct answer is a resounding "Yes!"

I hope you'll also think about the children that my students once were. I saw those little boys every time I stood in front of our class. If I don't persuade you to support programs for people in prison, perhaps you can help in some way to keep today's at-risk children and teenagers from trashing their lives and the society that belongs to us all. Maybe you can volunteer in a drug or alcohol abuse prevention program at a school or at a drug or alcohol rehab program for youth in your larger community. Maybe you can become a mentor or tutor or children's advocate.

Anything you do to help one person in prison or one child who's at risk ultimately will help us all.

15 *FBI Uniform Crime Reports,* www.fbi.gov/ucr/ucr.htm
16 Ingrid A. Binswanger, M.D., Marc F. Stern, M.D., Richard A Deyo, M.D., et al, *The New England Journal of Medicine,* 356 (2007): 157–165.

# APPENDIX B

Faith without good deeds is no faith at all. Hope without action is like lukewarm acceptance from those who claim to care, which is more bewildering than outright rejection from those who don't.

—Dr. Martin Luther King, Jr.

I n Appendix A, I promised you suggestions for action. This is neither an exhaustive or representative list, only a sample to give you leads and ideas.

- Almost all religious denominations have a prison ministry on a national program level. Local churches can give you program information.
- If you live within driving distance of a prison, you can get in touch with the volunteer activities coordinator at that facility and ask what they need. Some prison systems post volunteer opportunities on their state government Web sites. If you have ideas about a program you'd like to start, the volunteer activities coordinator is still the place to begin.
- Your sheriff's office can give you information on programs in your local jail.
- Both the sheriff and the chief of police are good sources of information for programs in the schools and community

that serve youth, recovering drug and alcohol abusers, and ex-offenders. The office of probation and parole, your local office of social services, and your United Way chapter also can help.

- I *do not* think it's a good idea for young people to volunteer in jails or prisons, but there are things they can do, such as collect yarn or other craft supplies so prisoners can make items for charities; collect children's books for prison waiting rooms or visiting areas; or collect books for prison libraries, prison hospitals, or inmates. Check with the volunteer coordinator before you start these efforts.

- These are two of the national programs that offer volunteer opportunities: C.U.R.E. (Citizens United for Rehabilitation of Errants), www.curenational.org and Volunteers of America®, www.VolunteersofAmerica.org

- I am available for consultation, talks, or workshops on this topic.

# INDEX

For Additional Copies, Check Your Local Bookstore, Order Online, or Order Here

Yes, I want _____ copies of *So Am I: What Teaching in a Prison Taught Me* for $14.95 each, plus shipping and handling.

Include $3.00 shipping and handling for one book and $1.50 for each additional book. Maryland residents must include 6% sales tax.

Payment must accompany orders. Allow 3 weeks for delivery.

My check or money order for $_____ is enclosed.

Name (Please print)_____

Organization_____

Address_____

City/State/Zip_____

Phone_____
E-mail_____


Make your checks or money order payable and return to:

A Closer Connection, LLC
P.O. Box 70
Owings, Maryland 20736

www.teachinginprison.com

Lightning Source UK Ltd.
Milton Keynes UK
UKOW01f1920070318
319078UK00001B/211/P